SISTER EMMANUEL

MEDJUGORJE THE WAR DAY BY DAY

Florida Center for Peace

The Publisher and the author recognize and accept that the final authority regarding the apparitions at Medjugorje rests with the Holy See of Rome, to whose judgment we willingly submit.
This book is published with the understanding that the witnesses contained herein reflect the personal viewpoint of the author, and are not meant to indicate the official position of the Catholic Church.

ISBN 2-84024-029-7

Burtin - F - 41600 Nouan-le-Fuzelier, France

Original Title: MEDJUGORJE, LA GUERRE AU JOUR LE JOUR
Translation: Juan González, Jr., Ph. D.

Published by The Florida Center of Peace

The Florida Center for Peace
P. O. Box 431306
Miami, Fl. 33143

MEDJUGORJE
THE WAR
DAY BY DAY

To the Queen of Peace, my mother and cause of my joy

To my Croatian friends of the village of Medjugorje

To my Serbian brothers who call themselves my enemies but who would be my friends if we had had the leisure to sit down together for some coffee and more than coffee.

PREFACE

I greet you, my dear reader, who have this small book in your hands. May peace be with you, may war and destruction of life remain far from you, from your family, from your friends, from your country and from all our humanity!

In this small book you will be able to read the information that came out of Medjugorje. It was sent by Sister Emmanuel who is a member of the Community of the Beatitudes. With three other young people from her community, she had the great courage to remain with us during these difficult days. Their presence was for us not only encouragement but also the hope that we would not be abandoned by our friends, by those who, like us, believe that the Queen of Peace speaks at home. It is also with affection that I would like to present this small book and to say a big "thank you" to Sister Emmanuel and to her community for their presence and for their help.

We experienced very often that our suffering was also their suffering.

We have been able to understand in this way what that means for us men having someone who is ready to share our suffering. Our sufferings did not disappear but they were easier to endure. Such is the sign of communion among us and with all the Church. With the growth of love our communion will grow and with the growth of our communion we will overcome all the sufferings and we will transform them so that they will be for our good and for the glory of God.

The news of our village which you will find in this book is a picture of the suffering and of all the destruction which occurred in our region. It is with recognition that we noticed that this information helped many of our friends in the world, all those who wanted to know what was happening at home. In this manner we were able to express the truthand that is important for liberty. That is why this information has represented a special fight against lies and false rumors which circulated on the subject of the situation in our region. To live the truth and to manifest it before others is our holy responsibility.

This truth has touched many friends in France. It has aroused much love, compassion and thus has permitted victims to receive an important help, expressed concretely in medicine and food. Here I feel compelled to say thank you in the name of all the poor and victims of war, to the Community of the Beatitudes. A big thank you also to all those who heard the cry of the poor, thanks to this community which has made the voice of the Gospel ring out.

In the same manner we circulated the voice of our Mother, Queen of Peace, who invites us to conversion and shows us the safest way to obtain peace. The message of peace will remain current even after the war because it invites us to love, respect, protect life and to stop destruction. The same message consists of an invitation to return to God the Father who loves each one of us.

And you, dear friend, if you ask yourself what can I personally do? This is the answer: begin to love your own life; thus, you will love the life of others and all creation. In this manner you will stop the most dangerous war. If you love life, you will be very close to the Mother of Life, the new Eve. It is she who will help you to discover the way to God and to the others. When you arrive there, then you will find the means to help those who suffer be they near or far from you.

May God bless you and may He be your peace! May the Blessed Virgin protect you and guide you in this earthly valley toward paradise, a place of eternal love and ineffable peace!

Medjugorje, at the beginning of the twelfth year of the apparitions,

Father Slavko Barbaric, ofm, Parish of Medjugorje.

Monthly message of the Blessed Virgin of March 25, 1992.

Dear children,

Today as never before, I invite you to live my messages and to put them into practice in your life. I have come to you to help you, and, therefore, I invite you to change your life because you have taken a path of misery, a path of ruin. When I told you, "Convert, pray, fast, be reconciled", you took these messages superficially. You started to live them and then you stopped because it was difficult for you. No, dear children, when a thing is good, you have to persevere in the good and not think, "God does not see me; He does not listen to me; He is not helping". And so, you have gone away from God and from me because of your miserable interests. I wanted to create out of you an Oasis of Peace, love and goodness. God wanted you with your love and with His help to make miracles and thus give an example.

Therefore, here's what I say to you: "Satan is playing with you and with your souls and I cannot help you because you are far from my heart". Therefore, pray, live my messages, and then you will see the miracles of God's Love in your everyday life.

Thank you for having responded to my call.

I
Beginning of April 1992: war breaks out in Bosnia-Herzegovina...

that evening...

The door opened with a bang allowing a panic-striken horde of women, children, old men to enter our chapel... it is the hour of complines, the hour when the hymn of the evening prepares us to spend the night in the great peace of God, but here the strident cries and some sobs come to interrupt our music. The time of lighten... and babies' bottles take place alongside our liturgical candlesticks, baby diapers bumped into our bibles. The floor was covered with plastic bags crammed with a thousand things which had been hurriedly gathered and, in the corners, they were already spreading out some blankets to make the old people sit down. Two or three radios, which were blaring out according to Croatian habit, roared the news.

It is April 6, 1992. It is 9:30 p.m. The war has just broken out in Bosnia-Herzegovina. We have to act quickly. Bernard and Maurice removed their monastic habit in order to carry some sandbags and to block all the openings of our cellar which was converted into a chapel. The people of the neighborhood know that our cellar is the best (not for wine!) in the district in Bijakovici. That is why they took refuge there. They examine all kinds of figures:

- If the bombs fall from the south side, then it is better to put the children to bed at such a place.

- If the bursts come from the north, then it is necessary to barricade the door. But then, how does one have access to the toilet? We discussed, we squabbled a little in the Croatian way (a lot of noise but little harm!) and between the two we remembered the Queen of Peace and we explained: "Majko moja!" (my mother). Some "baba"[1] quietly recited the rosary. The children at an age of not being able to understand are rather happy. All are going to sleep here together; it is better than at home, and the occasions for playing have multiplied by ten...

All the able-bodied men have rejoined their combat unit; some left for the front since this evening. Anguish already wrings the hearts of spouses and mothers: "Will he return?" At the house we are six; I must make the introductions!

- Milona von Habsburg, a German, has lived in Medjugorje for seven years and helps the Franciscans very much. She currently speaks five languages and often accompanies Father Slavko on his trips to assist him as well as the visionaries. Full time in the service of the Gospa.

- Nicky Eltz, an Austrian American, special secretary to Father Slavko, excellent photographer, has been in Medjugorje for four years, well known for his ingenuity in providing service in the most impossible circumstances.

- Finally four French, a little unit of the Community of the Beatitudes, who came to Medjugorje to enter the school of the Blessed Virgin in prayer, and to help French speaking pilgrims to enter into the spirit of the place.

•Cécile, age 24

•Maurice, age 29

•Bernard, age 32, and I.

The house was loaned to us by Bernard Ellis, a Catholic Englishman converted by Medjugorje and of Jewish origin, and by Sue, his wife. Without knowing it they largely collaborated in helping the village in the course of the war; we deeply thank them for it.

Then, that evening...

We moved some mattresses for the improvised dormitory, and already the mothers are sleeping next to their children on the same mattress in the Croatian manner.

---

[1] "Baba": 'Grandmother' in Croatian.

An unpremeditated detail: It was an orthodox Gospa (the icon of the Mother of God from Vladimir) who watches over all this little world terrorized by an orthodox enemy! A living prophecy of the reconciliation of the children of God...

Late at night the bells of the Church began to ring a full peal. It was a signal for an aerial danger. Our hosts recommended to us to sleep with them in the cellar, all stretched out in rows of onions. But we placed our mattresses underneath the staircase of the basement thinking of escaping in this way the continuous noise of the radio and commentaries...

After a solid white night and a difficult attempt at the Office of Lauds outside of our chapel - cellar - dormitory - refuge, I recommended to the brothers not to leave the house and I went to the Franciscans for news. The situation was clear; the Federal Army in the hands of the Serbs had begun to attack. It was only a beginning; one had to expect the worst. At thirty kilometers from Medjugorje, Siroki-Brijeg was already being bombed. And for an airplane, thirty kilometers is a distance which is quickly covered. We were not to go out of our homes.

Those who have lived a war know this experience. In record time, one has to make very grave and vital decisions and that with many unknown elements of discernment... my neurons collided in my head while my heart remained in a profound peace and told me that we did not have anything to fear.

The house was simmering with excitement. Several heads came out fearfully from the cellar while the husbands who had returned from their watch around the village began to give orders everywhere, with a Kalashnikov on their shoulder. Their voices trembled; for months they have been speaking of the war, they dig shelters in the mountains and practiced firing... But today it is no longer a rehearsal: the war is here for real and from now on the protection of Croatian villages, their lands, their families belongs to them alone. They tried to cover up their fear. We love them very much because they are our neighbors, our friends. For more than two years we have shared with them their problems and their joys and tears come to our eyes on seeing them leave thus for the front, with a broken heart. Their humility touches us very much; some entrust their women, their children to us "in case anything happens". All hang on a rosary on their left shoulder even our neighbor Drago who never goes to Church.

- It is all right. I tell him to encourage him, you take the Gospa with you; she will protect you!"

For the first time, he asks me to pray for him, and gives thanks like a kid who is a little embarrassed. Previously he used to spend his days in the game rooms of the Medjugorje slot machines and in a few hours the war will make him become again a child of Medjugorje's Queen of Peace.

Several women took us aside to drop a word in our ear;

-"Leave quickly today; the Tchetniks[2] are going to come here. They will kill you like the others. You have your families in France; go and find them. Here it is very risky for you... take the road toward Split and there you will perhaps have a boat. Be safe!

-We shall see... do not worry about us. The Lord and the Gospa will show us in prayer what we must do. We are here for them; they will show us then...

- But are you not afraid???

- No, we are not afraid. There is the Gospa; with her we are not afraid."

There is amazement on their faces! And the noise to spread like wild fire in the whole cellar, "They are not afraid; they say that they have the Gospa... No, no, they are not afraid!"

I send Cécile to buy the most bread she can if she still finds some and to gas up. Bernard wants to begin to pray but Maurice advises him rather to fill with water all the cans which he finds in the house because a water cutoff is feared. At the same time he was to cut boards in order to block all the windows of the ground floor.

Milona is absent for a few days. Nicky ate his breakfast with an Olympian calm while some mothers came to warm their feeding bottles on the gas cooker. I observed my three brothers and sister for whom I am responsible before God. The peace which wrung our hearts was unbelievable, supernatural. The war was necessary for us to experience at what point the peace of God was dense, compact, overwhelming and that it surpassed every intelligence. Each one leads a busy life with all his heart and supports with patience the evasive responses which I offer to his multiple questions.

- The gas, does one move it away from the house or does he keep it?

- Do we move all our things to the cellar?

- Do we fit out the rear of the bus with blankets and boxes of supplies if we have to evacuate the people? Who would drive?

How would he find the others if they have already left?

How much time do we have to prepare the boxes? What would we put inside?

---

[2] Tchetnik: this word in Croatian means "member of the group". For more than a hundred years, their objective is to destroy everything that is not Serbian in the regions near Serbia. The assassination attempt at Sarajevo before the First World War was the result of this idea. Today under the Communist mantle they pursue the same objective.

- Do we sleep here this evening or not?...
I have been in worse situations! One thing is for sure;
- "At eleven o'clock, the rosary on the second floor and a community meeting".

It was a kind of rosary video; we wanted to pray, we pronounced each phrase of the rosary forcefully, but in our imaginations all kinds of images and ideas passed. That led somewhat to this: "Our Father, who art in heaven, may your name... (an image of Josip in his bunker near the Neretva, who sees a horde of Serbs coming on him)... give us this day our daily bread... (an image of my mother who learns through television that the war has broken out here)... blessed art thou among women and Jesus... (an image of father Jozo who has been injured, under the debris of his monastery at Siroki-Brijeg, and the Gospa who comes to dress his wounds)... third joyful mystery, the birth of Jesus... (an image of the left tower of the church which was collapsing: Maurice hurries to save the Blessed Sacrament. Too late, he was hit by a splinter and falls with the ciborium, and the hosts were scattered...) forgive us, Lord! We were already on the fifth joyful mystery: Jesus is found in the temple.

As far as the community meeting, it was the shortest in our history. I only had two things to say:
"1- For years, the Gospa explained to us in her messages that we would know the Will of God in prayer. "In prayer, you will know what to do.", she said recently. Today we only have prayer to enlighten the course we are to follow. Our vocation here is unique; the Lord who has His plan for us will show us what to do.
For us it is the moment to live this message. Thus I ask each of you to put yourselves before the Lord and the Blessed Virgin during the next twenty four hours and ask them: Is it your will that I return to France or that I remain in Medjugorje? Each one of you is completely free to leave. We will drive you to Split without a problem. Only those who have received the conviction in prayer will stay.
2- If all of us ask to stay, we will entrust ourselves to the Divine Providence for our life here.
Yet, there will be a situation when we will be forced to leave. If the Tchetniks cross the Neretva and head for the village in order to take possession of it, it is

---

That is why in the actual language here every Serbian soldier is a "Tchetnik". But only God probes the bottom of hearts.

not worth the trouble to have four more victims. We will flee toward the coast, and leave to return later if the situation is calm.

For that it would be necessary for everyone to gather some things in his travel bag and have it at hand in case we would have to leave the first time. There is a sum of money for each one in case one of us will lose the others in the debacle. And constantly keep all your papers with you!

- And our friends who do not have a car, are we not going to abandon them?, asked Maurice.

- No, thanks to the van we will be able to make as many shuttles as necessary to Croatia."

That is all that I could tell them for sure, because for the rest our lesser landmarks were vanishing in our continued quicksands.

I found Nicky very thoughtful before the table in the kitchen. He finished writing a short report on the local situation this morning and he intends to send it by fax to the United States. That gives me an idea; I am going to do the same thing in French since I am inspired by his and I will send it to my community in France, to my family and to Strasbourg[3].

On that day I was at a thousand places thinking that I was writing thus the first page of this book, the first fax in a long series which was going to circulate like wild fire, day after day, during the war, besides tens of thousands of friends of the Gospa scattered throughout the whole world. I did not imagine for a second that my short papers, written in haste for my close relations and without any research and style would represent for the crowds of old pilgrims the only daily news coming out of a local witness, still living in this village dear to all and suddenly cut off from the world by the war. It is only later that I would learn that they were appearing from the following day in certain newspapers, that they would be read on the radio, that the Medjugorje centers in the world would be waiting to disseminate and arouse prayer movements and that even.... they would be faithfully piled up on a desk at the Quai d'Orsay.

Blissful ignorance on my part! I see there a gift from the Gospa; She has permitted me to serve her without knowing it, in great simplicity, and she has spared me from being taken for a journalist. This has spared me... many headaches!

In these pages do not look for a history book by a professional or a political vision of the situation in Bosnia-Herzegovina or still a scholarly description of

---

[3] Thanks to an answering machine, for a year now, I transmit twice a month news from Medjugorje to members of our association: "The Children of Medjugorje".

military movements, or even the well polished report of a journalist who would have spent his days in ferreting out strong impressions. You will find rather the spontaneous expression of a heart in love with the Queen of Peace and her Oasis which is Medjugorje; a heart which sees the village live, which listens to its suffering, its courage, its hope; a heart which tries to understand the

Gospa's plan through this drama and which shares in bold strokes what it sees, hears and perceives and the only objective to rejoin other hearts, themselves also in love with the most extraordinary village in the world.

News from Medjugorje, April 7, 1992, 1:00 p.m.

The town of Siroki-Brijeg (30 kilometers away) was bombed this morning. Four dead. Later two MIG airplanes were destroyed by the Croats. The Croatian forces are attacking the airport at Mostar at this moment. The Serbs responded to it by bombing some residential areas near Mostar and by threatening to "take" Medjugorje if they do not stop. Some planes have already flown over; the Croatians fire above. For the past twenty four hours the events have been moving fast. Here in the village everyone is in the cellars at the call of the bells from the church in case of an aerial attack. Every able bodied man is in uniform. Everything is well anticipated and organized and ready to move at the least signal.

Father Slavko preached a retreat of fasting and prayer to twenty people...

Pray, pray, pray!

Our hearts are in peace. Thank you for sending us all your angels! We will update you.

Peace!

P.S. Thank you for transmitting this message; our lines are functioning very badly.

To stay or to leave? (April 8, 1992)

That day I waited for an answer from my brothers. Did they receive anything in prayer? I took each one aside.

- I will stay, Cécile told me. I do not promise you to stay all the time. I must see if I can hang on but for the time being I will stay.

- Emmanuel, I have just asked for the grace to be able to stay, Bernard told me in a very emotional and solemn tone.

- And you, Maurice?

- What about me?

- Are you staying?

- If I stay.... oh, I forgot to ask the Lord! In any case it is clear; I do not know why one would leave just as things are getting hot! The people are going to need us.

As far as I am concerned, the conviction which was necessary for us to stay was so intense in my heart that I did not get to pray for it. I had the impression that the Lord was telling me: "Why do you ask me the question when I have already inspired you with an answer? "This conviction did not take away from me one single moment of the war. But in order to remain open to the Will of God, we were placing our decision each day before Him during prayer in the event that He would have a new indication to give us. For example, if the situation became very difficult for the one or the other, he would be able to leave for shelter in Italy or in Provence. It would be only for some time.

Jesus and Mary were truly our only sources of light. They have never abandoned us.

News from Medjugorje, April 8, 1992, 1:00 p.m.

Dear brothers and sisters and friends,

We are overwhelmed with such support on your part. We really feel it, for peace and joy do not leave us for one minute! A thousand thanks!

For the first time in Medjugorje the evening Mass was not at the church but in the cellar of the presbytery with blocked up dormer windows. The village did not suffer any attacks but from here we distinctly heard the bombs fall, undoubtedly in Mostar. The airport was completely destroyed by the Croatians. Thus Serbian planes could not move. The airport is in flames with its horrible MIG's.

At Siroki Brijeg, the damages rose to seven dead and some thirty wounded. (The area critically lacks doctors. In Medjugorje, the only medical authority is a very competent Irish nurse but she is all alone. Thanks to your help she has medicine, some instruments, but we would need a good doctor).

Combat continues almost unceasingly on the ridge between Mostar and Zitomislici. There are Serbian tanks on the main route passing along the east side of the Neretva. Some "snipers" (with telescopes) occupy the east side of its canyon. Trenches have been dug up and are occupied by men from Medjugorje both on the north side of Apparition Hill and on the area which separates it from Mount Krizevac. The village of Vionica (five hundred inhabitants), three kilometers from Citluk, has had some of its houses burned down by the Tchetniks.

1:15 p.m.

We have just seen a drop of bombs, luminous and very slow in the direction of Siroki-Brijeg. The planes do not pass above us but not far. We see them and hear them. Bombs over Grude and the village of Slavko.

Private: M.A., G.B., Y., Thank you for your three extremely comforting faxes. Continue to work to protect Bosnia-Herzegovina. If you still send this message, then please cite also the message from the Gospa (3-25) so that all understand well that it is through prayer and by living the messages that miracles will take place. Said the Queen of Heaven and earth in whom we place our trust for she sees everything in the light of God and she loves each one of as much as her Son Jesus...

Also say that everything that will be done to protect this region, will be done to the Blessed Virgin Mary for she has chosen Medjugorje to make it a source of grace for all humanity. She desires our help!

Be careful; false news in France: No, Medjugorje was not bombed.

News from Medjugorje, April 9, 1992, 10:00 a.m.

Dear brothers and sisters, dear friends,

Thank you for your ♡ and your prayers offered to the Lord for Medjugorje and all of Bosnia-Herzegovina.

Up until now, Medjugorje has nor received any bombardment and everyone is well. Here we have helped the evacuation of some children. Some continue today toward the villages next to Ljubuska. Those routes are without danger.

We often have alerts and we hear bombings but far away. Slavko tells me that the village of Krucevici (seven kilometers from here) was reached tonight but we do not know if there were any damages.

According to the radio, some planes continue to take off from Titograd in the direction of Bosnia-Herzegovina...

Vicka told us with tears in her eyes that the Gospa had a sad countenance. She did not add anything. She was waiting in prayer for the wave to pass. As far as I am concerned, I think that the crest of the wave is to come. Yesterday six bombs were found in Citluk but not exploded. Thank you, dear Gospa!

We have one of the best cellars in the village in that of the presbytery. We provide shelter to some of the villagers there.

Cécile, Bernard and Maurice told me that they wanted to stay with me. Peace is in our hearts. It is evident that if there is a Serbian invasion overland with massacres to support it (let us recall Croatia) we will flee toward the sea with a large number of children. We have a Peugeot 305 at our disposal, a truck and Milona's car. Gas is still available; the garage owner is our friend. We are not lacking any food.

It would be well for the Blue Helmets to set up in Medjugorje. It would stop the Serbs who have something against the churches with spiritual influence. The planes fly over us from very high and from far. The Croats are very well equipped to destroy them. I tried to keep you posted before this evening. Peace and ♡

P.S. Nicky helps me with the news which we have through the Franciscans, Josip and the soldiers from Medjugorje, straight from the front, plus the local radio and television.

Six bombs and three children (April 10).

Cécile has three little sisters: Geneviève, six years old, Catherine, age ten and Lucy, age eleven.

On April 10, she received this fax from her father:

"A little smile from heaven to the little children"

Wednesday evening (April 8) in the dining room, the usual evening meeting. For several days the rosary has replaced the decade. We explain to the little ones (attentive...): "Just imagine... we are loading bombs on a plane to go bomb other regions...all right... if you, who are little children, say your rosary, you touch the heart of the good Lord... and do you know what the good Lord does? He will drop the bombs on a deserted terrain... or even better He lets the bombs fall but He prevents them from exploding....

- It is true; can He do that?

- But of course...go quickly! We say our rosary and we go to sleep!

The next morning... the next morning... (Thursday, the 9th), Sister Emmanuel faxes us among other things: "Yesterday six bombs were found in Citluk but none exploded. Thank you, dear Gospa!"

We could hardly believe it... except the little ones who found it logical and normal!!"

Inspection in Citluk (April 9)

Maurice narrates...

That morning, Nicky forewarned us:

- "I am leaving for Citluk to take a picture of the famous bombs."

- "Maurice, do you want to go with him?" Emmanuel asked me. (She knows that living locked up makes my blood boil!).

My heart seemed to stop beating and I got immediately into Nicky's car to see with my own eyes what everyone feared; these deadly devices which our enemies sent against us. And then I needed a little adventure; I needed to leave this environment of fear which surrounded us.

My trust in God was more than real, living. I knew that nothing would happen to me. (Nothing to do with heroism, careful!)

The people of Citluk showed us immediately the location of the bombs. We arrived at a house; the bomb had fallen five meters from the wall. And it had driven two meters into the ground. It was a "cluster bomb", forbidden by the Geneva Convention (about 2.50 meters long; an ogival head, a tail with different kinds of wing tips, a body with different stages in which many other little bombs are found). Five or six military men were there and had surrounded the location with a red band. The job of diffusing had already ended but one clearly saw the multiple little bombs which could have been ejected approximately two hundred meters above the ground and scatter over a large radius causing enormous damage.

Nicky was impatient to see and to take pictures of the other bombs too. The second one had fallen fifteen meters from the factory; it had driven into the asphalt where the workers put up their bicycles....

The third bomb was twenty meters from a modern home over a little mound. Four or five soldiers were digging at the foot of a tree in order to free the bomb, and their blows fell some centimeters from the bomb... which was not diffused! I made a sign to them that it was extremely dangerous (risk of an explosion), but they answered:

- "It is necessary for someone to do it!"

(I thought of the precautions which one would have taken in France...)

Since the blows from the pick-ax were coming close to the bomb, Nicky and I did not want to make old bones in the area...

News from Medjugorje, April 10, 1992, 10:30 a.m.

Dear all of you who love Medjugorje,

A peaceful evening and night here in Medjugorje except for the noise of the bombs in the distance. Yesterday Maurice and I evacuated some children; we returned late and because of the very strict blackout, we were not able to go to fax to send you the news.

If there is any false news circulating, here is the truth:

- Father Jozo was not killed nor was any Franciscan.

- The bombs on the village of Slavko missed their target; no damage. We gathered the pieces of bombs in the gardens.

- No bomb has fallen on Medjugorje. Those we have seen were several kilometers from the village.

We are aware that they have aimed at Medjugorje. It does not date from yesterday but nothing has happened yet. Your prayers and fasting have had a lot to do with it!

This is life here: the men from the village spend twenty four hours at the front, then forty eight hours in their homes. The women get together in the cellars of their homes because everyone sleeps in the cellars. The children have been evacuated little by little with their mothers. We can no longer go to pray on the mountains. Ivan and Vicka have their apparition at home.

The Mass, the rosary and adoration take place in the cellar of the presbytery. The villagers who lived in prayer in the family, and whose heart was close to the Gospa, are in great peace. It is beautiful to see. Josip and his family have a form of thunder; they comfort everyone.

Anxiety was caused by threats made by the Serbs who have encircled three thousand Muslims in the north, near the Serbian frontier. If they have not given up their arms by noon, they will be decimated at knife point. The name of the place is Foca (twenty kilometers from the border). Pray so that the massacre may be avoided!

If you send this news in writing, also include one or two messages from the Gospa. It is She who has the keys to peace.

We constantly keep in touch with Vicka who spends most of her time in a cellar of Bijakovici, and who, of course, is a true light for us. Ivan is at home; he prays with his family. He did not take up arms. Neither of the two gives any special messages. The Gospa comes to pray with them and to bless us all. Did she not say: "prayer is the only means to save humanity."?

Thank you for your prayers and every concrete initiative which has come from those prayers. Thank you for your perseverance and your love!

Peace and ♡

News from Medjugorje, April 10, 1992, 8:30 p.m.

To all of you, supporters of the Gospa,

This evening after Mass Medjugorje is in peace. This afternoon the explosions coming from behind Podbrdo and beyond the Neretva River were strong and numerous. At six o'clock in the evening, all the Croatian troops of the area were unharmed. Neither wounded nor dead.

Maurice who was not able to stop himself from climbing Krizevac (He was indeed the only one!) saw the smoke rise from Mostar where the situation is more than difficult. Your powerful support and this great solidarity expressed throughout France and Belgium are a constant comfort to us. I convey to the Franciscans and the villagers who are extremely touched...

When one walks with God, one has as an ally, He who never loses the war.

Private fax to Florence, April 10, 1992, 8:30 p.m.

Dear Florence,[4]

This evening again Medjugorje is protected from every bombing but we hear explosions from the other side of Podbrdo, beyond the river...

Message from Josip: "Can you add to your truck for Otocac some medicine for the sheep which exists only in France: "Ristelan". The veterinarians should have some. When the sheep have a certain virus, their paws are paralyzed and that is contagious for the rest of the flock." They are afraid to lose their flocks. This is not really the time!

We have very good morale and for that thanks to all of you. We are in the hands of the Gospa; is there a better place?

Hello, Ephraim? (April 11, 1992)

The decision to stay in Medjugorje could be serious with consequences and as a shepherd of this mini-community I wanted to submit this decision to our founder. Obedience is a basic element of our life. I deeply think that thanks to it, a community can hold itself against winds and tides and avoid the dislocation in the midst of a society which extols, on the contrary, the individual will as the source of freedom.

Ephraim is a true father for us for if he often receives from God signs for such or such a house, he shows great trust in the proper grace of each shepherd to guide his little flock. For my part I knew that he had given me a free hand in Medjugorje. Yet having seen the gravity of the hour, I considered it necessary to consult him. Who knows whether the Blessed Virgin had not spoken to him for us...?

Not easy... His line did not answer and I had to give up on a phone conversation. It was then through fax that the matter was handled. I clearly explained the situation to him , the real dangers and risks and at the same time

---

[4] Florence de Gardelle has not stopped organizing humanitarian trucks since the war in Croatia began. One of our best addresses for the needs of the village...

what the Lord had already put in each one of our hearts. Here is his response on a fax, illegible in part, dated April 11, 1992.

"My dear Mother Maillard,[5]

These few words to tell you how I am and I live with you. I pray with my poor prayer for the victory of the Gospa over the forces of evil.

I am very happy that all have decided to stay. It is truly in these circumstances that one can prove his love for the Church in a personified way. I feel very united to you in the gift of yourselves. I feel that the strength (...partly illegible...). We are not abandoned.

I embrace you tenderly in the love of the heart of Jesus and Mary."

Ephraim

News from Medjugorje, April 11, 1992, 11:00 a.m.

To all our brothers and sisters and friends,

The strong explosions heard yesterday at the end of the afternoon were due to a rain of shells sent by the Serbs on the little village of Bivolje Brdo which was partially destroyed. This village is on the other side of the Neretva River not far from our lines guarding Apparition Hill, in an area comprising Muslims and Croats. The results of this morning were two dead and three wounded undoubtedly evacuated to Grude. This village is very near the lines of the men from Medjugorje and the shells fell approximately 500 meters for the nearest... Everyone mourns these dead, the first victims in our area. Thank you for having Masses celebrated for their souls and for all the victims of Mostar, Sarajevo... whatever their membership or affiliation be.

I state precisely for those who know Medjugorje that our lines are at approximately five kilometers from the village. One has access to them by a rocky road which goes around Apparition Hill and which goes toward the cliff of the Neretva River.

Medjugorje is calm. We are going to evacuate other children.

United to you in the burning heart of Jesus and Mary.

---

[5] His affectionate way of calling me.

Private: Dear Geneviève, Slavko 'stole the thunder from the papal Nuncio'. We will fax you the text as soon as possible. Please, add to the truck some K-Way for the soldiers; it is raining...

Private fax to Vincent, April 11, 1992

Dear Vincent,[6]

Everything is O.K. with us; we try to make ourselves useful. Each one has his function: Bernard, prayer; Maurice, the most precious activities of resourcefulness in times of war; Cécile, my right arm for a thousand tasks, plus the peace at home which she marvelously keeps, and I... a constant "happening" between the sending of news, the needs of the village, contacts.... At the moment I feel like a very poor computer in which they have threaded some very powerful programs!

Do tell the whole family that the best residence for anyone is where the Lord wants him. Now, I am not even touched lightly by the idea to leave this guard post (When the Lord wanted to make me move, He always knew how to tell me clearly). The "3" also decided to stay with me. We will leave only in case of massacres, but everyone here says that the Serbs cannot come to the village overland.

We have a super cellar but that is nothing compared to the powerful angels whom the Lord (in His foreknowledge of my life) judged indispensable to furnish me. Tell mamma, mummy, and company... that I embrace them and that their complete trust in the Gospa is more than precious to us.

One thing strikes me: in a few days, throughout this war, some crowds have focused their eyes on Medjugorje, a task which we were not able to accomplish in ten years... God makes use of everything. The nuncio had an idea. If the Franciscans in Medjugorje wanted to send a message to the Holy Father, he would be able to hand it to him in the days which followed. Preparation for action, then, at the presbytery because it was necessary to act quickly before the departure of the nuncio for Rome. Father Slavko wrote the letter in Croatian, and between two visits from soldiers, he dictated it in German to Milona who among several phone calls, dictated it to me in French.

---

[6] My brother in Paris.

I am responsible for making the final copy in French, and Cécile of typing it. We could not find any headed note paper... exactly the day on which we must write to the pope! The most difficult thing was to make each priest sit down for a minute to countersign the letter. The excitement at the presbytery was at its peak that day, and the time of the rosary was very near... afterwards it would be too late.

Medjugorje-Rome by way of Paris, April 11, 1992

A "Child of Medjugorje" from Paris informed me that she has just had a long conversation with the Apostolic Nuncio in France. She had the joy of confirming that he loved Medjugorje very much. He confirmed to her, on the other hand, that on his part the Holy Father was very much in favor of Medjugorje, in a private way, of course, for as pope he could not officially make a pronouncement before the Commission of Bishops which has been appointed for that purpose.

Here is the text of the letter:

Your Holiness,

We greet you sincerely from Medjugorje, the place where crowds of pilgrims have gathered these last ten years, have prayed for peace, have converted to God through the intercession of the Queen of Peace.

We thank you for all you have done for the Croatian people up to now. We thank you also for having recently recognized Bosnia-Herzegovina. Very grateful, we express to you our profound trust and we assure you of our prayers for you personally and for all your intentions.

Now we turn to you, Your Holiness, at this very difficult moment of our history. After the recognition of Bosnia-Herzegovina, the Federal Army, the last Communist army in Europe, began and savagely continues destroying and annihilating villages and Croatian and Muslim towns. This has resulted in many human victims.

Great is the suffering of these innocent people. Ravno, Kupres, Mostar, Bozanski Brod, Foca, Zvornik, Visegrad, are some of these places. There already exists a real danger for all Herzegovina of the west. We, here at Medjugorje, hear the loud explosions daily. The fighting is already very near. The first bombs have also fallen on the territory of the parish of Medjugorje. Thanks to God, up till now, there have been no human victims. People are in panic. War planes fly over us. We take refuge in the cellars. Many have already left their homes and live the life of refugees. Because of this constant danger, we have also closed the parish church through which millions of pilgrims have passed and have found there the way to God through prayer and the intercession of the Queen of Peace. We celebrate Holy Mass in the cellar.

Most Holy Father, in this difficult misfortune, we turn to you. We beg you to want to knock on the door of the conscience of all the responsible people in Europe and in the world through the great authority of yours everywhere so that they react immediately and stop this aggression never before seen on innocent people of Croatian and Muslim nationalities.

Very grateful for everything that you will do, we greet you sincerely and we wish you all the good possible. On our part, we assure you of our prayers and our fasting for the plans of peace in the world.

Medjugorje, April 11, 1992
Friars of the parish house of Medjugorje

II
Mid-April, 1992
A Holy Week
unlike the others...

News from Medjugorje, April 12, 1992. Palm Sunday, 11:00 a.m.

Dear brothers and sisters and friends,

Grace and peace to all of you!

For the first time since the beginning of the war, we spent 24 hours almost in peace at least as far as Medjugorje and its near accesses are concerned. That is good! Since I am not a journalist, the information I send you concerns only our situation in Medjugorje and, of course, its surroundings.

Some villagers equipped with olive branches gathered around the cellar of the presbytery, indeed very few for this Sunday Mass.

One does not see a single child on the streets of Medjugorje... the homes are empty for the most part because of the mass exodus for Makarska and Split. Here we see only the soldiers guarding Medjugorje who come to rest between their tours of duty at the front. Almost all of them have a rosary fastened to their epaulets.

We have four visionaries present.

Ivan, who goes to pray on Apparition Hill every day in spite of the danger. The men of Bijakovici did not want to give him any weapons. They said: "Your function is to pray, not to fire."

He himself would not have wanted to take up arms. He sees the Gospa every day at his home at 6:40 p.m. She shows him how much she is with us "I am with you", and how much she sympathizes as mother. Vicka is active in order to lift the morale of the troops. She enlivens prayer in the cellar. Ivanka is at her home in Miletina (three kilometers from the church) with her two children. Milka, Marija's little sister, who saw the Gospa only on the first day of the apparitions and who takes care of her old parents.

With respect to the pilgrims, Vicka told me: "It is better for them to wait until the situation is straightened out." Some wanted to come for Easter.

Before the atrocities shown on television and all those which will remain hidden, many of you feel powerless. Nothing of the kind! Whatever one's age, health, conscience, faith be, each one is important in the accomplishment of the peace plan of the Gospa. She has said it! I beg you; read her messages and see. She has the key to peace and she explains to us how it is going. This peace that the world cannot give. Each one is as important in her eyes as a political leader. How? Hatred comes from Satan, but the least one among us can reduce him to powerlessness through his personal efforts of forgiveness, reconciliation, love... a simple rosary, fasting which is difficult; that means a bomb that will not fall on a village. It is the arm of hatred that is paralyzed...

Thank you! Thank you!

11:35 a.m.

A loud noise from an explosion over Siroki-Brijeg but the target was missed.

Private: Dear Gildas, your network is super; I am proud of you!

A Jewish mother (April 13, 1992)

A "Child of Medjugorje" informed me that she would see Cardinal Lustiger (Paris) in two days and that she would deliver him some of my faxes on Medjugorje. Knowing the deep attachment of the Cardinal to his Jewish roots, I add for him these little known details about Medjugorje. An exceptional fact in the history of the apparitions, the Blessed Virgin expresses herself in a strange language to the visionaries and this language is her own language. Marija Pavlovic was the first to explain it to us.

- "Sometimes the Gospa speaks in a language that I do not know. One day I asked her in what language she spoke and she answered me: "In my mother tongue". It is Aramaic".

We then recited to Marija the Our Father and the Glory be to the Father in Hebrew as well as the Shema Israel to see if she recognized these prayers.

- "No, I do not recognize them. In any way, I do see that at that moment the Gospa is saying some spontaneous prayers. One day I retained some words and since there was a priest with me who understood Hebrew and Aramaic, I gave him these words after the apparition to see if he understood them.

- And was he able to translate?

- "Yes. The Gospa was saying to God: "I thank you for having created them."

Yet, that rarely happens. We have been able to observe that the Blessed Virgin prays "in her maternal language" especially when persons of Jewish descent are present or persons who are closely tied to the people of Israel.

This peculiarity of the apparitions of Medjugorje represents an important sign for our times and it is not by chance that the "Virgin of Israel" appears today as a Jew. In fact she stresses thus discretely but clearly the important place reserved for the Jewish people in the accomplishment of her plans for the world.

Vicka was also asked.

- "Yes, sometimes the Gospa prays in a strange language that I do not understand.

- And have you asked her what language it was?

- No, why?

- It would be very interesting to know...

- Oh, you know, when I need to know something, the Gospa explains it to me on her own. I do not need to ask her any questions!"

A touching simplicity... We understand better why the Blessed Virgin has chosen to appear to Vicka rather than to a brother from the Beatitudes... She is more peaceful!

Unfortunately this information has not yet been able to be sent to Cardinal Lustiger. If one of the readers could do it... thank you! And not only to the cardinal but to every Jew who is waiting with an open heart for the signs of the times for his people.

News from Medjugorje, April 13, 1992. Monday in Holy Week, 10:00 a.m.

All of you friends of the Gospa,

Yesterday, two bombs over Siroki-Brijeg, but no wounded. They missed the target. From here we heard the noise, and two minutes later the television announced the results. In the afternoon, the four of us went to Podbrdo to pray. The sirens in Citluk sounded several times.

Yesterday evening, for a solid hour, lots of bombs over Citluk. Our house trembled. Once again, the cease-fire was not respected! A spotting helicopter flew over us a part of the night. I do not know yet what the damage is in Citluk in terms of men and buildings. I will tell you as soon as possible.

Yesterday, the famous Muslim Croatian village of Bivolje Brdo, which had been bombed and which had been fortunately evacuated, was invaded by the Tchetniks who killed the animals and stole whatever they could find in the homes before setting them on fire. They were followed by their trucks to carry away their booty. Yesterday I saw Vicka here in her cellar which is rather a shelter on a hillside. "There are, she says, ten or eleven inside. Some "babas" (grandmothers) and some girls." It is so small that I ask myself how there can be so many: 3.5 meters by 3 meters, approximately 1.8 meters high, without windows, entirely on concrete, a little electric radiator in the center... Fortunately the Croatians are used to sleeping in numbers in very small rooms and they are heavy sleepers. Vicka is always so radiant!

How do we thank you for your support! Continue especially in your efforts of prayer and different sacrifices like fasting... You can do so much for us; let God do the miracles that He wants to do!

Peace!

Private fax to Jean-Marc, April 13, 1992

(Regarding a project: to conduct a massive campaign to request Milosevic to spare the "Gem of Medjugorje".)

Dear Jean-Marc[7]

Let us be careful and do what the Gospa has entrusted to us, and not fall into

---

7. Berger, from our house of Saint-Broladre.

the trap of encroaching upon other activities, not bad in themselves but which have not been entrusted to us by God. God has entrusted them to others. The petitions, for example, are not our business. The Gospa has asked us to live and to spread her messages not to initiate petitions. And then, let it be said between us, I do not believe at all in petitions to change the heart of a man who plays into the hands of Satan. I believe only in prayer. The more you arouse him with petitions in favor of Medjugorje, the more aroused he will be against Medjugorje. That is the psychology of the Evil One... we cannot take this kind of person head on. (He makes me think of Hitler in some respects.)

This is a personal opinion but be very sure to act according to your conscience.

Vicka and Fear

With the greatest spontaneity in the world, the visionaries at times utter words of a shocking profoundness. These last months, Vicka has often told us that she would not leave the village unless the situation in the country would be resolved. In order to challenge her one of us asked her:

- "But, Vicka, are you not afraid? And if the Serbs invade the village?"

Without even reflecting a second, the intense and clear look:

- "You know, when we have God, when we have the peace of God in our hearts, what can we fear?"

News from Medjugorje, April 14, 1992. Tuesday, Holy Week.

Praised be Jesus! (It is the greeting in Medjugorje and always the first words of the Gospa when she appears).

Dear brothers and sisters and friends,

The situation is really worsening. We do not have yet any Blue Helmets here or in the surrounding areas, and the enemy continues his machiavellian plan with all impunity...

Yesterday two bombs fell over Capljina (17 kilometers from Medjugorje), behind the Krizevac chain. Toward 6:00 p.m. I left for the rosary. I saw one of the bombs fall behind Krizevac; 400 meters to the left of the cross, there were some luminous fallouts. They aimed at the church but it escaped destruction as well as the hotel and the water reserve. There was one dead and three wounded. When the planes flew over, the aerial defenses reacted immediately limiting undoubtedly new efforts.

In the village of Livno, next to Siroki-Brijeg, a friend of Father Slavko was murdered in his home by a Tchetnik.

The Franciscans asked all the foreigners to leave as a security measure. There is a small group of about ten in addition to the four of us. They did not ask us to leave.

Vicka and Ivan always have their daily apparition. Yesterday Monday, the Gospa appeared for Ivan's prayer group. Ivan said that her countenance was very worried; he sensed a deep suffering in her. Since one of the members had to leave for the front (the guitarist, Vicka's brother-in-law), the Gospa thus advanced the apparition to permit him to join the prayer before leaving for the front. Such is our Mother.

All four of us are doing well. The Gospa shows us in peace what we must do.

Yesterday I repeated to Vicka to what extent you were in prayer with us. I explained to her what you were doing so that peace would come. Then with all her heart; she wrote to you these few words in Croatian:

Dragi Prijatelji!

Hvala od srca za vaše molitve, i žrtve
što činite za nas u ovom trenutku.
Mi smo svi dobro. Budimo sjedinjeni
u molitvi molimo jedni za druge.
Obilje Božjeg i Gospina blagoslova i mira
uz Bomoć Kraljice mira, i njezine prevelike
ljubavi za sve nas. Puno vas sve voli
i pozdravlja vaša

Vicka

"Dear friends, thank you whole-heardedly for theprayers and sacrifices that you are doing for us at this moment. We are all doing well. Let us be united inprayer; let us pray for one another. Over you the abundance of blessings from God and the Gospa; over you peace with the help of the Queen of Peace and her great love for all of us. I love all of you and I greet you, yours, Vicka".

Private fax to Geneviève, Tuesday, Holy Week, April 14, 1992

Dear Geneviève,[8]
(who expressed her desire to come to Medjugorje with two more people).

The situation is worsening. This morning the Franciscans packed their liturgical things undoubtedly to put them in the shelter. Act according to your

If the massacres come closer, we are headed for Split. If some morning you do not have any news, it is that we are in Split or rather that the telephone and the fax lines are not in service.

Forgive me for the telegraphic aspect of these messages... my heart is heavy, heavy...

Private fax to Vincent, Tuesday in Holy Week, April 14, 1992

Dear Vincent,

Everything is going well for the four of us. Reassure mamma - the Gospa shows us from time to time what we must do. We have never felt ourselves so much in her hands. It is an unimaginable experience.

The car is ready to leave for the sea in case the Serbians make a breakthrough. Then we would have 24 hours before us to escape. Do not be especially concerned!

---

[8] Genvieve Bastard was our "Paris connection", very active in the cause of Medjugorje.

conscience but my sisterly advice is that you should not come, except the doctor. The parish is asking all foreigners to leave (not us, wow!). That really caused many...

Interview with Vicka

Sister Emmanuel: What do you feel facing the Serbians? Do you pray for your enemies?

Vicka: Of course! When the Gospa asks us to pray, it is for all men whoever they may be. We must pray for the Serbian people although they are doing this to us. If we do not show them that we wish them well and that we are praying for them, if we do not set the example of forgiveness and of love, then this war will not end. The most important thing for us is to try not to get vengeance. If we say "he who has done me evil must pay, and I will do the same thing to him", this war will not end. We must forgive and say "God, I thank you for what is happening to my people and we pray to you for the Serbians for truly they do not know what they do."

Sister Emmanuel: In this village of Medjugorje, is there hatred?

Vicka: I know many people who are not capable of love toward the Serbs. They would like to see them as far away as possible from them. But I would like to say to these people not to think that way. Because if the Croatians think thus, peace will never come! We must wish the Serbs well and pray for them. May our prayer be able to touch their hearts so that they understand that this war is leading nowhere.

The Blessed Virgin has often told us that the war was the work of Satan. And Satan is so powerful that he wants to confuse our thoughts in every way possible. Especially now he is extremely active.

Sister Emmanuel: In what can we help you?

Vicka: In a number of ways! We are not asking for military help but if you can give us medical help and food that would be good. And speak to others about our situation so that they can help us in return.

We pray for you in recognition of everything that you are doing. Everything that you do with the heart, with love, is a help against the war.

News from Medjugorje, April 15, 1992. Wednesday in Holy Week, 11:00 a.m.

Dear brothers and sisters, dear friends,

Praised be Jesus who on this Wednesday of Holy week walks with lucidity and love toward His passion in order to save us. He is weeping over Medjugorje and the entire Bosnia-Herzegovina just as He wept over Jerusalem.

But we can greatly console Him. He can still work miracles for these people. I am going to make myself the spokesperson of the Gospa. Read and "live my messages"... "Through love, dear children, you will obtain everything." (See "Words from Heaven").

We continue hearing explosions here and there. Yesterday our forces shot down a Serbian plane which was attacking from Capljina, at 7:00 o'clock in the evening. Then at 11 o'clock in the evening, our forces shot down a Serbian helicopter which was flying over Citluk. Undoubtedly it was the one that had annoyed us all night which followed the so called cease fire in flying over Medjugorje in order to establish points of reference. In our sector, no victims. But let us pray for all.

Why aren't there any Blue Helmets yet? Do not wait until there are some dead everywhere for you to make your entrance, please. It is now that we need you!

I attach the text written by the Franciscans which stresses the point of yesterday's situation.

We remain with you in the great mantle of the Gospa and in the burning heart of her Son our true and beautiful abode.

Peace. Thank you for everything that you are doing... what a comfort to us!

Truly some courage?

Since the first weeks of the war, a leit motif often came to the mouth and the writings of our neighbors with respect to us.

- "What courage you have!" And this noise only causes it to increase. That is why I today wish to let the beautiful sound of the bell of truth ring and bring a fatal blow to these hasty interpretations.

Of course it is true that the four of us have suffered from this war. First of all through our communion with these people, beloved and torn apart, but also through the internal attacks of Satan who evidently wanted "to eliminate us from here" (as he wanted moreover to eliminate the entire village) and who made us feel it with some particular keenness. We easily recognize his paw but if that was really painful to us, we would only be comforted by the idea that our presence in Medjugorje pleased God.

As for the courage, that is something else. From the beginning to the end we have benefited from a completely astonishing grace; not one of us has ever felt fear. That could come only from on high and we will never be able to bless the Lord enough for this gift. Queen Esther showed great courage, because she had had to overcome her fear to be able to save her people from extermination (confer Esther, IV, 17).

For us it was different. Having been exempted by God from this terrible load which is fear, the sacrifice would have meant for us not to stay in Medjugorje but, on the contrary, to return to France. To abandon Medjugorje at a time when the village was living these very crucial moments for the plans of the Gospa, so crucial then for the future of the world! We were experiencing with enormous calm a spiritual battle over this village; we were becoming an integral part of it and to remain there was not then a sacrifice for us. Then, where is the courage?

I am going to tell you where I have seen true courage. I have seen it especially among the men of this village, the days when it was necessary to leave for the front and where the anguish made their lips pale. They were getting up without having been able either to eat or drink such were their insides closed up. They would crowd together in their poor trucks while trying to look good. They could not even hug their wives and their children, because the latter were on the coast living in the hotels for refugees. When they arrived on the mountain, they spent whole nights watching, in the humidity, the mud, huddled up in their small shelters which resembled rabbit holes and where they did not have any place to move. A permanent risk of being wounded, captured, tortured or at best killed. Noise from the planes full of bombs. Explosions unbearable to the ear and the heart, noise from the shells above their shelters. Courage for them consisted of faithfully returning to the front, to walk over their fear, day after day and week after week to be able simply to defend their families, their homes and their lands; to protect us, us who were sleeping dryly on good mattresses.

I saw the courage in our friend Josip who, to protect his people and his land, spent a whole night so close to enemy positions that he heard the Serbs breathe. He knew that the least error on his part, the least sneeze, would be fatal to him.

I saw the courage in our neighbor Ankica, mother of many young children who [illegible] never left the village and who lacked everything. I will never forget the last look full of love, modesty and of tears which she cast on her poor husband weakened by alcohol when she had to leave him for an undetermined amount of time - three weeks, a year or forever? - and to leave alone with her tribe by bus to the other end of Croatia where no one was waiting for her, with her rosary and her faith as only supports. So many mothers have had to do the same thing!

The silent courage of the poor is so beautiful, so profound, that I can only cry when I recall it.

News from Medjugorje, April 16, 1992. Holy Thursday

Dear brothers and sisters, dear friends

Praised be Jesus who today delivers us His Body and Blood with such love!

Today, a lot of news with respect to the near accesses to Medjugorje. Each one is on his guard but, except for certain artillery rounds which were heard yesterday evening, nothing special has taken place.

Of course, you know the ultimatum presented by the United States to the Serbs for April 29? Are they going to be held accountable for it? We are waiting to see it with our own eyes!

May our prayers and our offerings of love serve so that the responsible politicians may be inspired and that consciously or unconsciously, they accomplish the Gospa's plan of peace. This plan which comes from On High, which is perfect and which does not flow from human logic. For this war is, first of all, spiritual; Satan wants to intensify hatred in order to better destroy the children of God. His goal is not only to give us death in this world but also eternal death. The Gospa has explained all that to us very well for almost eleven years. The true weapons, the most effective ones, are in each of our hands, thanks to prayer and to sacrifice.

Dear Gospa, we wish to raise the level of love and lower the level of hatred, with you, so that murderers can no longer capture their satanic inspirations and that their plan of death breaks up inwardly. Such is the power of the disciple of Jesus!

This evening we commemorate the Last Supper in our little community and we will do the washing of the feet in communion with all of you.

One sole ♡, one sole soul in Jesus our Pasover. Peace!

Private fax to Geneviève, April 16, 1992

Dear Geneviève,
(Following her request for the number of victims)

We cannot have here any number concerning the victims in Bosnia-Herzegovina. I can only tell you that as far as the extended parish of Medjugorje, there are no wounded and no deaths. As for the rest... the Croats are already having problems inquiring exact numbers in time of peace; imagine then in times of war!

A family letter addressed to our supporters. Medjugorje, April 16, 1992

Dear Children of Medjugorje and all of you who love the Gospa,

The war has come upon us like the flight of grasshoppers on a wheat field. Since April 6, Bosnia-Herzegovina has been put to fire and sword by the Serbian troops. Sarajevo has become a new Beirut; Mostar is being bombed, and as in Croatia, the churches are the first targets of the destroying airplanes. If in France the press still obtains information in Belgrade (capital of Serbia), you are not risking being up to date on the tragic situation which is ours in these days.

At the end of January, while washing the dishes, Marija had confided to me: "The war is going to come to Bosnia-Herzegovina." I had tried to erase this word from my spirit, but on March 25th, since the last message: "You have chosen a path of ruins...", I understood that it was imminent.

Today Medjugorje rings with the noises from bombs which are attacking Citluk (6 kilometers) and Capljina (17 kilometers).

All the able-bodied men -our friends, our neighbors. The children have left with their mothers; their laughter and their games have left the streets of Medjugorje to make room for the strident noise of the anti-aircraft guns. This place that you have known in all splendor has become devastation and we are not at the end of our sorrows. It is the time of trial for the Croatian people, chosen, selected among many by the Gospa to receive her most beautiful manifestation in all history, since her Assumption.

We understand better why the Blessed Virgin wept on the third day of the apparitions while begging:

"Be reconciled, be reconciled!"

The hatred which has been opposing the Serbians and the Croatians for a very long time already pierced her heart and already rung the alarm of this series of atrocities.

Oh! If we had only listened to her voice of a mother and walked with all our heart in her beautiful plans of peace!

Today it is Holy Thursday, the day on which while giving His Body Jesus "loved us to the extreme". In receiving this Body of my Spouse, I would like to ask forgiveness of my Croatian brothers for having taken lightly the messages of their queen and our queen and for having thus participated in their agony. Pardon from my Communist Serbian brothers for not having obtained their meeting with God through my supplications as Catherine of Siena would have done... I ask forgiveness from the Gospa, the treasure of treasures of Medjugorje, for not having known how to do away with the distance between her heart and my heart and for having thus allowed the enemy room to come to destroy.

It is not too late. "Pray, live my messages, she tells us, and then you will see the miracles of the love of God in your daily life." (3-25-92) I begin today; today I decide for prayer with heart and for true conversion.

We can unite ourselves and thus help the Gospa with all our strength to bring victory over hatred and over him who inspires it, Satan, the destroyer.

Here is my proposition: Go to the front with Vicka's brothers, Marija's, Ivan's... Not while slipping with them into the trenches of Apparition Hill but in us fighting to the death against the sin which still lives in us. But in praying and fasting with the heart. But while we huddle under the large mantle of the Gospa, with rosary in hand pray in communion with Vicka who from the bottom of her sordid shelter, watches over Medjugorje with a smile that already belongs to heaven.

Thank you, thank you! Peace.

The bells of the night

Cécile narrates...

Ah! Unforgettable are the first nights which we lived at the beginning of the war! It is with a smile that I think again today, of those sudden awakenings, in the midst of a dream, to the sound of the bells of the church which rang the signal to warn the village of imminent danger.

They had forewarned us of the different signals which these bells could give:

- If they rang for one minute, we had half an hour to get to the shelter (The planes then were flying out of Titograd.)

- If they rang for more than three minutes, the danger was imminent. The first time I woke up in a jump at the sound of the bells.

With anxiety, I asked myself:

"That makes how many times they have been ringing?

Is that more than three minutes? Did the brothers and sisters hear them? Should we go down to the cellar?

If so, what should we take, my toilet case, my flashlight, my travel bag (prepared to leave at full speed if the Serbs arrived), my papers? Will we be able to go to our room if the bombings are intensified?

Do I have the time to brush my teeth? As I am getting dressed, I am in pajamas or I put on my pants to be able to run faster if I am pursued? If I wake up Emmanuel and if it is a false alert, it is crazy for once she has gotten up, she will not be able to go back to sleep..."

After this avalanche of thoughts, I go out like a whirlwind into the corridor, my things under my arm. There I come across Emmanuel who asks me:

- "How long has it been ringing?"

And, before my ignorance: - "Quickly, wake up the brothers, every one to the cellar!"

On his own Nicky is already on the terrace with dishevelled hair, scanning the stary sky waiting for the least sound which would indicate aerial danger. He fires at us:

- "Come on! Keep cool[9], one does not even hear the planes! For my part, I will not go down to the cellar, that... never! Good night!"

We decide to obey the bells even if, like Nicky, we all prefer a quick death in our rooms to an agony of several days under three hundred tons of reinforced concrete.

That was a very bad night...

News from Medjugorje, April 17, 1992. Good Friday, 10:00 a.m.

Dear brothers and sisters, dear friends,

Blessed be Jesus for "there is no greater love than to give one's life for those whom he loves..."!

Yesterday at the hour of the parish rosary, an event which had not taken place in Medjugorje for years: the apparition was public. The whole assembly was very close behind Ivan, in the cellar of the presbytery which had become the only place of worship since the war. The apparition was particularly long and Ivan told us its main points. The Blessed Virgin prayed for a long time over us and she blessed us. Ivan entrusted to her all the intentions of these people, who have been torn apart, the families, the victims... She said: "Dear children, I call you to perseverance in prayer. Dear children, since the beginning of the apparitions, I have told you that through prayer and fasting you could stop wars.

[9] The presence of Nicky has often helped us not to dramatize the situation when danger is threatening.

That is why, pray, pray, pray." Then the Blessed Virgin prayed a long time with Ivan for peace.

Yesterday we heard the bombs all afternoon. An attack over Neum, near the coast. As for the village of Stolac (30 kilometers), consisting of Muslims, Croatians and Serbs, it was partially burned down. The Tchetniks put the torch to many of the Croatian and Muslim homes. The horror continues with all impunity...

Through a miracle, Medjugorje is always preserved. Those who are still here leave their cellars little by little to sleep in their homes. By day, several "baba" venture to do the most urgent tasks in the fields.

Vicka tells me that the countenance of the Gospa has been the same since the beginning of the war; it expresses suffering. Ivanka left a week ago for Zagreb. Marija has left Italy for Louisiana (USA) to undergo medical tests there.

We thank you from the bottom of our hearts for the extraordinary chain of prayer and solidarity which you form around the Gospa and Medjugorje these days...! Peace!

10:00 a.m., Holy Saturday

P.S. Yesterday's fax did not go through; we were cut off. No electricity, water no doubt for some time. The only fax which has a chance of functioning is that of the Franciscans, thanks to their electrical generator.

I am preparing for you today's news... not good at all.

Pray, pray, pray!

Life after life?

Yes, death roamed everywhere in the country. Especially for unbelievers, this reality was unbearable. We were seizing the least occasion to comfort one another while insisting particularly on the words given here even to the visionaries by the Gospa concerning what is awaiting us after death. Marija had rightly come to speak to us about that, at the house, just before the war. The Gospa actually had shown her heaven, purgatory and hell so that she would indeed understand that life on earth was only passing and that she may be able to give witness about that before so many and so many of our contemporaries who think that there is nothing after death.

(On her part, Vicka had thus asked the Blessed Virgin:

- Is there reincarnation after death?

- No, reincarnation is a pure invention of man. After death there is eternity.")

Marija spoke to us first of all about purgatory.

* Purgatory

"The Gospa showed us purgatory but also heaven and hell. She showed us that so that we would know that another world exists. Many people think that only our world exists and that afterwards there is nothing.

When we saw purgatory, we saw like a cloud, a large cloud. We were not able to see the faces, but we heard the cries of those who are there. They asked us for our prayers; the Gospa recommended to us to pray and to make sacrifices for these souls so that they can go to heaven faster..."

* Paradise, an increase in happiness

"I saw it like a great space. There were many people there. They were all dressed in long robes of different colors. These colors do not exist on earth but they resemble blue, white and pink. All are very happy. They thank God for everything that He has done for them in the course of their life for they see again clearly their life on earth and everything that God did there. There is a crescendo; they understand better and better the Will of God and also know God more and more. God is so great that they never get tired of knowing Him more.

When we say in the creed "I believe in the Creator of things visible and invisible", we say it in faith without seeing these invisible things. But in paradise, they see them and they always understand them more. In paradise there are no more secrets; everything is an open book.

Where we went we did not see God. Only the people who were in paradise. When Vicka and Jakov went there, they saw many meadows and flowers."

* Hell, a free choice

With respect to hell, the Gospa said that those who go there are those who have decided of their own free will to go there.

With the freedom God gives us, we can decide ourselves even against God.

The Gospa told us that they cannot go out of hell because it is willingly that they decided against God and they reject our prayers. That is why she has asked us to pray very much for sinners while they are still on earth. Because afterwards, when they have decided for sin, they no longer have the desire to be converted. Once in hell they no longer have the desire to be converted. Thanks to our prayers, the Lord makes some overtures to them in order to be able to convert them on earth but they are free to reject. The Gospa calls us to make a consecration of our lives for the conversion of sinners as the priests and so many religious do..."

News from Medjugorje, April 19, 1992 Easter Sunday, 11:00 p.m.

Very dear brothers and sisters and friends,

Christ is risen, alleluia!

The feast of Easter very crowded and intense here in Medjugorje. The priests say that the confessions are extraordinary specially on the part of the soldiers (of whom many did not come to church). This evening, the apparition with Ivan was again public in the cellar. The Mother of God is with us behind the sandbags... We live some incredible moments where each one opens his heart as never before. The village has transformed itself also inwardly.

Medjugorje is still completely intact, but from Good Friday at noon until yesterday evening we lived in the constant roar of explosions. Capljina (17 kilometers) is greatly damaged; there are more than 35 dead without counting the numerous wounded. I will never forget my Way of the Cross on Krizevac this Good Friday: the continuous explosions would tell me that at each station there were new dead, new agonizing, from the other side of this same mountain and I saw the mushrooms of smoke...

Father Jozo is doing well. He and his priests are very active in helping the people and hardly have the time to come to the shelters! The Italian Caritas has brought some help; the French arrive tomorrow.

We do not have any more water, electricity, fax, or a telephone. I had this fax sent by the brothers from the Oasis of Peace who are returning to Italy. We will see whether we are able to fax from Croatia especially for the message of the 25, which the Gospa will give perhaps in Louisiana (USA) which will be translated in Medjugorje to disseminate throughout the whole world... thank you, thank you for your prayer; the Gospa is about to carry out an extraordinary work. Let us love her more and more! We are very united to you in her ♡ Peace!

P.S. Sarajevo has become a hell; people hide themselves in their homes out of fear for their own neighbors in their apartments.

Interview with Ivan (April 22, 1992)

Ivan is waiting for us near his home. He asks me not to have the interview last very long because some planes had passed by half an hour ago and risk their returning. His countenance was grave but peaceful. He spoke slowly with the heart wishing to express his thoughts with the greatest depth possible.

Sister Emmanuel: "Ivan, what has the Gospa said these last times? Did she speak to you about the situation?

Ivan: The Gospa did not say anything in particular about what is happening at this moment. She is calling to peace. In order for peace to become a reality, it is very important that it take place in the heart of man. For if there is no peace in the heart of man, there is no peace in this world. If peace is in danger in a people, concretely, for example, in the Croatian people of today, it is in danger in all peoples. That is why we must particularly work on ourselves in order that this peace will take place in us and that we may be able to carry it to others. If peace does not awaken in man, there will be no peace in the world.

Sister Emmanuel: How can we do it?

Ivan: With respect to this, the Gospa invites us to relieve our hearts of many things. We must reject sin so that this peace can come so that our hearts can be open to the gift of peace.

The Gospa has been calling us to prayer and conversion for eleven years. She calls us to fasting and to sacrifice, to a strong faith and finally to love. It is all of these things which comprise peace.

Sister Emmanuel: How do you interpret the events?

Ivan: As a man who observes the current situation, I say that this war which is going on, is a conflict between good and evil, a struggle against Satan who, today in a very special way, acts through the intermediary of man. Men are imprisoned by hatred; they do not know how to love.

On the other hand, we say that this is an aggression of the last Communist bastion in Europe. It is fighting for power, for the privileges which it had before and which it does not want to let go. It has invested everything in this objective.

The Croatian people are not the aggressors; they are protecting themselves. They are defending their lands, their homes, their survival. That is why the whole world must be united so that good wins over evil, so that it is peace which will govern.

God has given the power to all the presidents of all the republics so that they can use this authority on behalf of good and not evil. That is why they can do enormously so that peace will come everywhere in the world.

Sister Emmanuel: Do you see sadness on the face of the Gospa?

Ivan: Listen, these days of Easter, in a special way, have been the days of a sadness... of a sadness! The Gospa was at the foot of the cross; she was in communion with everyone. Still today she is with us all who live here.

The Gospa spends the greatest part of the time (of the apparition) praying for peace. She is in communion with all of us who live this.

Sister Emmanuel: Do you think that the pilgrims will return some day?

Ivan: From all sides, people call me. From America, from Italy... they want news and hope to return because they are thirsty; here they receive a food which means very much to them. We are going to pray... whatever will be the Will of God, that is what will be".

Private fax to Nathalie, April 23, 1992

Dear Nathalie,[10]

Miroslav came from Zagreb and he put on a video cassette for us. Among others there were two excellent interviews: the one with Vicka and the one with Jozo on the current situation. These are historical documents. I made it a point to have them speak in Croatian so that they could give the best of themselves and they had a super warmth.

Miroslav will send you the originals; it would be super for you to make an editing with the best sequences (one would leave the Croatian in "voice off"). For someone who is not a camera pro, he handled himself well. But say that these "rush" are a true treasure for Medjugorje, its supporters, its history! No journalist has yet dared to come unless perhaps one or two in a quick superficial visit.

---

[10] Nathalie is in charge or our apostolate "Video Lumière".

Interview with Father Jozo (April 23, 1992)

Father Jozo has drawn features. He is constantly on the go and hardly sleeps. For months his monastery has been threatened with destruction by anonymous calls, and today, there are no longer unfriendly phone calls but the real noise from the bombs. The men of his parish are all at the front and come to consult with him willingly for some advice. With what care he receives them! He is a little their Moses. The victory of the army on the plain... from his arms raised in prayer is going to depend

He is very happy to see us.

- "You have stayed? It is good. All the others left; they did not need to. Now more than ever it is here that we must be."

- "Are you not afraid?"

- "No..." He laughs. "Nothing will happen to you. They are not able to do anything against Medjugorje. They will never break through the Neretva."

He speaks almost in a low voice as when he is praying or when he makes his words in the course of his conferences rise from a distance.

Sister Emmanuel: Was Siroki-Brijeg bombed?

Father Jozo: Yes, one morning while the people were asleep some planes flew over and dropped their mortal load on us. The bombs fell between the houses and the people were killed in their flats, in their homes. They are now without homes. There were seven victims and a large number of wounded.

Sister Emmanuel: How was the war able to begin here?

Father Jozo: The war did not begin here. The war had already begun on the earthly paradise with the first sin of man. Here ends a great war which in Europe began with the arrival of Communism.

Here, the prophecy of Fatima, with respect to the conversion of the world and of the debacle of the atheistic communist regime is justified, is carried out. And here where communism and evil were perhaps the most deeply rooted, here where the Gospa appeared for ten years, here is taking place what is going to be unique, grandiose: the victory, the triumph of the Immaculate Heart of Mary, the downfall of human errors, the change of the human heart, the creation of a new mentality, the beginning of a better world. Here, on this little territory where for several centuries already three great communities, three religious persuasions, have gathered and live: Catholic, Muslim and Orthodox.

The power was won at the elections in Serbia, in the Orthodox part of this church. It was won by the communists and those who wage war against the Croats, who are democrats and Catholics and against the Muslims. In other respects in this war we experience a great possession of the heart of man by evil, hatred, something rare, never seen in the preceding wars. With what hatred people kill, massacre their neighbor! At times even the members of their families who do not think like them.

Sister Emmanuel: How do you see the political situation? Do you think that the Croatians can conquer?

Father Jozo: Currently the political situation in Bosnia-Herzegovina and in all of Croatia is terrible. The politicians of the world regard the Serbian Army as the power with which to discuss even if no one has voted for it. This army does not represent anyone. That is why the violence of this great army, one of the most powerful in Europe because of its armament, is concentrated on a small area. All this technology and this evil on the area of our Republic of Bosnia-Herzegovina. Tons and tons of explosives, dozens and dozens of arms and munitions threaten us. We are the target and the victims of this war. The political situation is frightful because the democracy for which we have voted and desired, to which we have a right, is not protected by the great powers. It is left at the mercy and the disgrace of powerful, of armed politicians, of Communist generals. And it is sad!

Yes, the Croatians are going to conquer not only in so far as Croatians but as bearers of a democratic thought which will develop. The Croats will conquer because God will fight for us. God commits Himself for us. We feel in our midst how He is fighting for us, how He saves us and protects us like the Israelites who were leaving Egypt for the promised land. This same God, on the side of our prophets and our Moses, leads us truly miraculously through all the misfortunes and all the sufferings which we have confronted.

Sister Emmanuel: Can you tell us what the deep spiritual meaning of this war in God's plan is?

Father Jozo: This war in God's plan? God never wishes the war. God announced the war against evil, with her heel the Immaculate Virgin will crush the power of the dragon, the power of Satan, the power of the serpent. That war is not ended; just like the temptations of man have not ended.

But in this war the Church is cleansed. It is freed from the power of its errors, its weaknesses and its falls. In this war the Mystical Body of the Church reacts clearly. The whole world experiences, with the Croatian Church which suffers, this terrible war, this unjust war. The whole world hastens to help, to alleviate our suffering; it prays for us and with us. Throughout these ten years that have passed, the "Gospa" has prepared the hearts of so many men to love us and to feel close to us.

And when we have been attacked by the enemy, when the force of the Evil Spirit appeared, all of you recognized: There it is! There are the messages! The Gospa said: "Satan is strong! Drive him away through prayer, fast and sacrifice." She calls again so that as a Church you will show again your love and your faith through prayer, fasting and sacrifice for us.

Sister Emmanuel: How do you interpret the message of March 25th?

Father Jozo: God and the Gospa have tried to make an Oasis of Peace here and among the Croatian people. That does not mean that she has not done it, that she is not going to do it. The process has started; it is about to be accomplished. What we are living is the cleansing of the Oasis. It is the eradication of evil in the Oasis. Do you understand? This war is a settlement of accounts with a certain evil which has been planted here for fifty years, "the time of communism".

The last message teaches us that we had not sufficiently understood the messages of the Gospa. We did not sufficiently receive the powerful word of the Gospa. But when man is powerless before such an aggression, before such a force of bombs, mines, weapons, then man sees his limitations. He experiences how it is dangerous not to serve God until the end. In the last message the Gospa challenges us. She means that it is not to late to cleanse this oasis of peace from every disorder on a long term basis. You must help us at this moment. God has wanted to do great works with us; show us His power of miracle by us and through us. But He is not able to do it today. Why? Because in order to do that, He needs prophets who believe firmly. That's it. One cannot make a value judgement on this war and say that it is a negative fruit of the apparitions. How can one say that? The cross of Jesus was not a negative fruit on the part of Jesus vis-a-vis His Father. The cross came because of the presence of sin, because of the evil which Jesus found on earth. The apparitions of the Gospa arrived exactly when a great evil was concentrated in the communist world. Europe was not aware of this violence of evil, and today, it is becoming aware of it. It was such violence for seventy years in these territories of the Communist countries. Terrible violence. Now the whole world is aware of it.

Sister Emmanuel: Have the Serbs threatened your monastery?

Father Jozo: The Serbs? The officers of this ex-Communist army are not the representatives of the Serbian people. Today they want to threaten and they have already been threatening for a long time for on February 7th, 1945 they destroyed everything here and killed 758 believers in the parish of Siroki-Brijeg. Later they killed thirty consecrated friars of this monastery. Imagine, thirty friars from a single monastery! And this same army, this Communist army has threatened to destroy again, to sweep us away from the face of the earth as it did 47 years ago.

Sister Emmanuel: Can you tell us what we can do for you?

Father Jozo: First of all we must all receive the Gospa, her call, her messages; live her messages so that the stability will return to the Oasis of

Peace, so that this joy in the heart of man will return, so that the aggressor as well as his forces will withdraw from here.

Then, I would like to say: The Federal Army threatens us with military aggression. Now it would be necessary for American and European politicians to put pressure on the enemy and by not giving him more arms, not allowing him the possibility of spilling blood, massacring, carrying out a genocide over us. It is necessary to oppose all that, stop aggression.

It would be necessary to give us more room because we have been living in the heart of Europe for fourteen centuries. We are a European people. We have suffered aggressions. We are the heritage of European culture and an important part of its history. Europe should show some interest with respect to us; allow us more room within its programs, speak of events and of life in our Church, in our people and thus develop in the hearts of all, a responsibility toward those who suffer and the victims of aggression.

It would be necessary for all nations who have recognized the independence of our countries to do so in a way that democracy will survive with us and that we be preserved from elimination. Because of the document that the representatives of certain countries wrote, of certain republics and which they sent to their embassies was not sufficient. Now it is important to preserve peace and neither we nor the Blue Helmets are in situation to do it. We would need a comprehensive political school to put pressure against our aggressors who use the army for their sickly ambitions. These are the politicians who want to transform history, the historical frontiers, who desire to eliminate certain peoples and to make of them at least minorities, inferior people and slaves. We have been in this way during this whole century under Serbian power and its domination. And now we expect from you to be able simply to live in peace and in freedom like the child expects from his mother her protection, her help, her advice, direction, security, friendship. We also expect that from Europe.

Sister Emmanuel: When there are alerts, do you go to the shelters?

Father Jozo: Yes! It has been a long time since we have lived underground because we hear almost permanently this sad call from the siren inviting us to flee, to abandon the earth, to enter into the cellars, the shelters. I think that there is not a sadder call for man to whom the face of the earth has been offered, than to leave it to look for shelter, to look for a space in the cellar. It is a great humiliation for the man of our times facing brainless people in whom all intelligence is found in armaments, in the dust.

It is tragic to hide away children, parents, young and old, innocent people, people whom we take out of ruins and whom we take to the cemetery because we were not able to stop the take-off of these airplanes which are filled with bombs to deposit on our heads. That is why I would like to really ask all men of good will, to dress our wounds and to console us with their love, their interest for us, their responsibility, their humanity, their philanthropy. Because we can change the face of the earth, we must change the face of the earth. The Gospa is really looking for such partners: "I wanted an Oasis of Peace."

Now France can no longer wash its hands, excuse itself of not knowing that here the army massacres, kills, burns, destroys bridges, makes people powerless for generations and generations. No one can say now the he can innocently give weapons to such people or spare parts to allow airplanes to fly and to bomb again. It is very sad to listen to the radio or to discover ourselves that on the remnants of grenades and bombs are found inscriptions in French, in Swedish, in Russian...

Sister Emmanuel: What do you experience in your heart with respect to the Serbs? Are you tempted not to forgive?

Father Jozo: I experience a terrible responsibility and the need to show my people the grace of this moment. The Croatian people, Catholic, has found itself before a destructive power. Satan has taken our neighbors and has made them into our enemies. And they have become a cross for us: persecution, suffering, killings, annihilation... But on this cross, everything as Jesus prayed: "Father, forgive them!" We too must pray and we pray. I have met such people that have found the strength to pray for their enemies, for their conversion. I, in my heart, pray exactly for that. It is in my soul that I experience the greatest victory of Croatia. And that will be our final victory. As Christians and as believers, we go before our God and before our Church, before our conscience, to be able, with the deepest sweetness, with love and full awareness, to pray for our enemies, our persecutors, for those who hate us and persecute us, to pray for them and for their conversion.

Even this morning before everyone I prayed the rosary for this intention. And every day I give this intention: that God may illuminate the hearts of our enemies so that they recognize in us their brothers, their neighbors, whom they will love and respect. It is the work of the Church to preserve this attitude, this way of thinking truthfully.

Sister Emmanuel: The Gospa said "Be reconciled, be reconciled"... Does that affect the reconciliation between Orthodox and Catholics?

Father Jozo: You see, here it is not the Orthodox. It is the atheists. We cannot say that our enemies are the Orthodox. No, these are Communists who had privileges. They are... they do not know what they are. They are possessed by the lofty idea of being able to attain a large state. We cannot say that Hitler was Protestant or Catholic. No! He was a man who was possessed! The generals committed the Serbs and the Serbs followed them in order to create a great state. That is why this is not a war of religion. They hate everything in the same way. Now they hate even the Muslims. They do not admit losing some of this territory which they have ruled for a hundred years.

Not for a single moment did they give us the possibility of being a state, of being a people with its culture, religion, history, with its fourteen centuries of life in the Church, of membership in the Church, in the Catholic world. They denied that to us; they suppressed it.

That is why it is not a matter of a conflict between Orthodox and Catholics. No. It is an aggression from a remnant of the Communist regime, of a criminal.

Sister Emmanuel: Do you have a final message?

Father Jozo: To all those of you who are perhaps going to listen to these words, watch this broadcast, you who want to help us through prayer, I would say to you, as a form of conclusion, that the Gospa does not ask the United Nations to send thousands of soldiers. No army establishes peace, stability or harmony.

Peace is, above all, a gift from God which we must first of all obtain in prayer, a gift which flows from a heart which forgives. A gift which must conquer hatred in the heart of our enemies, conquer the evil in the hearts of men. But this evil cannot be conquered without prayer. Satan cannot be conquered by any weapon if it is not through fasting and prayer.

That is why I beg you: begin to pray for us and to fast for us. Pray with us and fast with us. Thank you because this way you are going to help to make the Oasis of Peace in Croatia live again. Then all of Croatia will be an Oasis of Peace and, through it, all of Europe, all the Church and the whole world.

Thank you because you are going to respond to our call, to the call from the Gospa.

A walk to Ljubuski (April 24, 1992)

In Ljubuski I had a beautiful friend, Drago, the postmaster. One day he saw me standing in line before a telephone booth caught among 15 Croatians (who do not have the same appreciation as we with respect to the minimum distance to keep between persons!). Understanding that I was French, he had invited me to his three star office to use his private line and to refresh at the same time his recollections about France. Our friendship had begun thus.

Drago came immediately to my mind when Nicky said to me:

- "Slavko has an urgent message for France. He wants to go to Paris. It is necessary for you to urgently fax Geneviève so that she may make arrangements for his stay.

- Let us try Ljubuski!"

It was dangerous because the enemy aircraft was prowling... but Nicky drove faster than a professional pilot. I also said to myself that the matter would be handled very quickly. In other respects, his angels are almost as effective as mine - pardon me, as effective as mine - that is not saying very little!

We were not successful in finding out whether the fax had been sent to Geneviève. And at the end of an hour of courageous efforts, we turned back. The car had hardly started when the piercing noise of the siren filled the air. Nicky drove along to Medjugorje at full speed because the planes were already appearing in the sky. Five minutes after our departure, the bombs were raining over Ljubuski on the same avenue on which we had parked...

Thanks to the angels!

Monthly Message of the Blessed Virgin of April 25, 1992

Dear Children:

Today also I invite you to prayer.

Only by prayer and fasting can war be stopped.

Therefore, my dear little children, pray and by your life be witness that you are mine and that you belong to me, because Satan, wishes in these turbulent days to seduce as many souls as possible.

Therefore, I invite you to decide for God and He will protect you and show you what you should do and which path to take.

I invite all those who have said yes to me to renew their consecration to my Son Jesus and to His heart and to me, so we can take you more intensely as instruments of peace in this unpeaceful world.

Medjugorje is a sign to all of you and a call to pray and live the days of grace that God is giving you. Therefore, dear children, accept the call to prayer with seriousness. I am with you and your suffering is also mine.

Thank you for having answered to my call.

A message obtained after a great struggle (April 25, 1992)

I will never forget this evening! As on every 25th in the evening, Father Slavko gathers several people who want to help in the translation of the message before sending it to the whole world. Since Marija is in Italy, it is by telephone that she sends the message. But Bosnia-Herzegovina does not have any more telephones, or fax; this makes it necessary for us to go to Croatia, to Vrgorac where the priest has a telephone.

You should see the expedition! Our friend Jean from Switzerland agrees to drive us in his little car. Because of the blackout, his headlights are covered allowing only a thin streak of light. In the back I was squeezed against Father Slavko. The road was filled with holes for several kilometers and the lack of light prevented the driver from seeing them far in advance with the result that our wheels did not miss practically any! Are we going to get to Vrgorac this evening? The route winds its way in the mountains and at each turn, I fall on Father Slavko and vice versa. Father Phillip Pavic[11] who had come for the translation in English, seats enthroned on his seat with his typewriter resting on his knees. He prays the rosary with us in all the languages, Croatian, English, French...

Obviously the priest is not at home. We look for him; time passes... provided he has not forgotten!

Italy does not answer. Slavko keeps his calm. He tries again without getting tired. He knows that this evening, April 25, the whole world is in suspense for the arrival of the message. He knows that after it has been hardly sent, thousands of telephones will get into action to spread the message as well as the minitels networks, computers, printing presses.

He knows that the whole night these words which have been received from heaven through an extraordinary gift of God will multiply at breath-taking speed, will enter into hundreds of thousands of homes to nourish the hearts waiting for light and comfort. He knows that because of the war the message of this evening is being waited for with unrivaled impatience. Is the Gospa going to say something about this conflict? And for the first time in the history of Medjugorje, is the message going to be blocked because of the lack of telephone lines?

Finally Marija's voice is heard but very poorly. Slavko repeats each phrase of the message over a little tape recorder and Marija who hears it confirms each

[11] He knows several languages well but his strong American acccent makes him really speak American in all the languages!

word of it. Everything went along well, at least one would think so! And we say good night to Marija.

There is no longer electricity in this city; therefore, it is necessary to type the message by candle light. Father Phillip has placed his typewriter on the table, an indescribable, old-fashioned piece. He tells us that he bought this typewriter in the 40's and that it has the advantage of carrying with it the symbols of all the languages. He begins by typing the Croatian; that takes some crazy time because we do not see anything with the candles. Toward the end of the message we see that the battery of the tape recorder was up to its tricks and that it lacked a phrase... it was necessary then to call Marija again!

Same old story immediately with the telephone. Patience, patience... that is it, we have the phrase and it is really: "Your suffering is also mine". The key word in this beautiful message which had to disappear. We translated in English, French, Italian, and German; each one looking at his neighbor's copy in order to come out with his translation. There is a problem with German; we had to call Milona in Munich.

Every language was typed a little slowly. It was very late; it was necessary to go fast to the post office to send the faxes. The manager at the post office had been told ahead of time that we would come well after the closing. He had to watch as we arrived. It was exceptional; the Gospa, the war...

But the fax machine was working very badly. It was necessary to attempt ten times to make the least number. I looked at these little scraps of paper containing some heavenly words which do not get into the machine... My heart melts; in such humility does the Lord carry out His divine work in the midst of His people!

That is it! Strasbourg's has just gotten through! And after some new efforts, America's! Thank you, dear Gospa!

Question: When this evening, you received the message on a silver platter, would you doubt all that had been behind it?

News from Medjugorje, April 27, 1992

"Oh, how easy it would be for me to stop the war..." (December 1991)

Dear children of Medjugorje and all of you who belong to the Gospa,

Thanks to the Gospa for the message of the 25th so strong and so clear, so loving and so full of hope. What army general would have dared to publish thus with such power of conviction the means which she has found to win the war with certainty? She needs to be called the Queen of Heavenly Hosts! Thanks to those who live with all their ♡ this genial strategy, this strategy of love which was explained to us to conquer Satan and his enraged growls.

We are always alive here in Medjugorje! All the nearby towns have been bombed ten times: Citluk, (6 kilometers), Capljina (17 kilometers), Ljubuski (13 kilometers), Grude, Siroki-Brijeg, Metkovic... human losses are among the civilians, even children. On Thursday the 23rd, eleven MIGS bombed Capljina; our homes here vibrated. The sky was sprinkled with balls of fire (not Pentecost, no, but the balls of heat destined to divert antiaircraft fire). Our forces destroyed six of these MIGS, and the result was that the bombings have calmed down a little. But the Croatians here say that it is only a part of them. Our men in Medjugorje always watch in their trenches; no one has yet been wounded in spite of the tons of grenades and bombs which have fallen over them above. All of them recognize where it is coming from, or rather from Whom the protection comes.

The big question remains: Are the Serbs anticipating razing Medjugorje? They have said it; they have even stated that Medjugorje would be their "dessert". Let us pray so that the Gospa may not only deprive them of dessert but also that she may pastor them of their cynicism of which they display evidence in these combats. The last strike of the tail of Communism in Europe. Marthe Robin had indeed prophesied that Communism would disappear from the earth.

In Medjugorje, we adapt our lives to the lack of electricity, water (fortunately there are the cisterns of old houses), telephone... Gasoline and gas can still be found when one makes arrangements with Croatia. Many of the refugees from Mostar and from Capljina have come here and to the poor villages of the surrounding area. Food is now lacking in some places. That is why we invite those who would have trucks to come and bring food as Paul Imbert has done, and the Community of the Beatitudes will be responsible to have it taken to the villages. The route along the coast does not present any problems, and if you are afraid to come to us, you can come to leave your merchandise with the parish priest at Vrgorac (between Makarska and Ljubuski). We will go to look for it. Vrgorac is a city in Croatia 33 kilometers from Medjugorje. Father Slavko left on the 26th for a tour of several days in Switzerland and in France. Father Jozo is doing well. He says that this war is a time of purification for Medjugorje and the Croatian people. He insisted to me that the Tchetniks could not enter Medjugorje.

Vicka and Ivan, the only two visionaries here, always have their apparition at 6:40 p.m. They say that the Gospa has a grave countenance and Vicka stated that She takes all the time of the apparition to pray with her for peace. Vicka has an astonishing radiance.

We have not seen yet any Blue Helmet or any force of deterrent military power capable of driving the Serbs to return to their homes. The ultimatums and threats on paper do not impress them. But God always draws good from evil; only He can do that.

We unite our prayers and our hearts to yours so that His holy and divine Will may be done and that none of His children will be lost.

April 28, 1992

Yesterday, the dispatch of the fax failed...

In order to better respond to the request of the Gospa in the message of the 25th, we can say with the heart the consecration to Mary of Saint Louis-Marie Grignon de Montfort or that of Father Maximilian Kolbe there is also a consecration to the Sacred Heart of Jesus of Paray Le-Monial, or the very beautiful prayers of Sister Faustina to Jesus. There are some prayers given by the Gospa to Jelena's prayer group which are found in the book "Words from Heaven" (Editions des Béatitudes, p.181) or every other spontaneous consecration done with love...

The peace which is in each of our hearts does not come from this world. Look at the design above: how it is good to live everything for the Gospa and to be enveloped in her mantle of love which is also the best of shields. Oh! May our prayers with her draw all men under her maternal mantle!

A thousand ♡ to all!

III
May, 1992...
... What are Europe and the United Nations doing?

False news

The continuing false news which came here was for us a very instructive demonstration of what the human tongue can give and also an endless source of jokes among us under these circumstances when we had few occasions to relax.

Living in the village, it was easy for us to compare rumors with facts. Here are some examples which we recall as we smile:

- "The Community of the Beatitudes was afraid to such an extent that it had to leave Medjugorje" (source from Italy). According to rumors, we have often left Medjugorje and we were asking ourselves how we could leave it so often without returning to it in the meantime.

- "Father Jozo was killed" (source from Belgium). For a dead man he still speaks with a lot of warmth!

- "The church has been bombed; there is no longer a stone upon a stone" (source from America). The poor church, it has been so often bombed in their imaginations that we ask ourselves how it is still standing!

- "Vicka is dying" (unknown source). For a dead woman, she is hiding her cards. We only see her at Bijakovici encouraging everyone to prayer and to complete trust in the Gospa!

- "Hurry up and flee from Medjugorje. The Serbs have a plan for the village. They are about to encircle it. In 24 hours it will be too late!" (source from... Singapore!) We always knew that the Asians had advanced technology but also powerful binoculars; we did not expect it!

- "The stained glass windows of the church are broken. Can you go and see if some have been spared and which ones?" (source from the United States of America). They are all in excellent condition, thank you, and you?

- "Medjugorje is in flames" (from London and other sources). This statement has given rise to so many rosaries and nights of prayer in the world that Medjugorje has been really scorched... by the flames of the Holy Spirit!

We were expecting to learn from one day to the next from a confidential communiqué coming from the interior of Australia that the Gospa had just been wounded in the course of an apparition, that she had been evacuated urgently to a temporary hospital in Citluk and that because of the lack of appropriate surgical equipment, her condition was becoming worse every hour...

Our friend Bernard Ellis received the original text of my faxes in England. He had them translated and disseminated them throughout the world with the help of a very well organized network. He expresses to me today his surprise each time that information returned to him after it has made its long journey through several continents. For example he stated: "A bomb fell a kilometer from the church" (exact) and two days later, it became "some bombs fell right on the church which is completely destroyed". Certain well-intentioned souls thought that adding to the passage a little touch of the dramatic, would result in more prayers... and then a kilometer; that is far!

It is true that the false rumors started off admirable movements of prayer. If we can deplore that the truth has been distorted, the Gospa had still profited from it because every prayer made with the heart pleases God and these prayers will have brought help in other terribly tragic circumstances which, at the time, were unknown to all. For example, the beginning of the "Ethnic Cleansing", with all its retinue of tortures and murders.

News from Medjugorje, May 1, 1992 Saint Joseph the Worker

Dear Children of Medjugorje
Dear supporters of the Gospa,

Blessed be Jesus and his adopted father Joseph who earned his daily bread from Him Who is the Bread of life!

Two days ago we saw the arrival of the first two trucks of the Blue Helmets. Four men will stay in Medjugorje. Tomorrow, six others will arrive; there will be ten of them. Their leader is French. ("There are twelve of them in Mostar; the others are in three other towns. That makes it then close to forty.) Still others will arrive. Divine Providence has humor besides love. They are lodged at the house of our neighbor who comes to sleep in our cellar with his mother and his sister. And so at the first serious alert, all ten Blue Helmets will come to take refuge with us!

But this presence has visibly changed nothing in the plans of the Serbs. All night we heard the bombs over Capljina, some around Citluk, so once again our window panes have shaken. Around 11:30 p.m. they were bombing Mostar in such a way that Cécile and I could see from our house the sinister illuminations of explosions which were flashing from the valley of the Neretva. And it continued this morning.

The truck with supplies from Saint Broladre (France) arrived well yesterday; a thousand thanks and love to them. The distribution began. Other trucks are being prepared. Especially preserves and food for the babies.

What is the Lord saying to us in prayer? To stay in this place in the service of the Gospa; first of all through prayer and fast and communion with all of you, and also through work and diverse concrete efforts. "Courage, Zorobabel... let us work!... Do not be afraid!... The glory to come from this temple will surpass the old... and in this place I will give peace." (See Haggai II,2-9).

Yes, let us work! (This is the day to say it!) Today, the Gospa counts those who have said "yes" to her and she is going to rely on them very much. It is with them that she is going to bring the victory and to accomplish her plan begun at Fatima. Through the rosary and prayer with the heart, she shows each one his task. What joy, yes, what joy for us to have her as our mother and to work under her direction. Thus, to have the peace of Jesus in our hearts!

Thank you; thanks to everyone!

When Saint Joseph drives a Peugeot...

It is impossible not to tell you the story of our 305. At the end of October, 1989, when Ephraim, our founder, decided to send a small delegation of the Community to Medjugorje, I had had to attend to all the practical aspects of the matter. For that I knew an excellent address: St. Joseph. On November 9, he received a little message from this old client that I am for him:

"Dear Saint Joe, you know how much I love you. In 9 days it will be the 11th anniversary of the day when I married your Son. So, if you are looking for a gift to give me, do not look any more. I am going to explain it to you.

I am leaving for Medjugorje to enter school and in the service of your spouse, the Gospa, because she is inviting me there. But you see, it will be very difficult to be down there without a car. I will be stymied by the least thing. Therefore, it would be really terrific on your part to offer us a car, to her and to us, a car to help the plans of peace. I know well that in Nazareth you and she did without a car but times have changed and I know that since then you have learned how to modernize. We would need a good car-four seater, solid, easy to maintain because I am not a mechanic, with a good trunk. Avoid a car with two doors; we get crowded in the back. A four door one is better (it is important to give him all the details). I have exactly the time to make a novena before the 18th, and since this 18th falls on a Friday, it would be really terrific if I could announce to the brothers in the evening, during the Shabbat, that I have the car. Imagine the praise which would ascend from their ♡ In other respects, do not go beyond the time of the novena for granting it, for it is the last date to be able to prepare the papers before our departure (scheduled for December 1)".

The following two or three days, I had some doubts at times. A mean little voice suggested to me: "If you think that you will have your car on the 18th... you are dreaming!" But I had told all the brothers of Mortain of this novena beforehand, and many had decided to participate in it. I decided to opt for a blind trust in the help of Saint Joe. I had so often experienced his care!

The days went by... Friday came and nothing in the horizon. But in the afternoon, someone gave me a letter from our monastery at Nay written by our Sister Marie-Raphael who was going to leave with me.

"Dear Emmanuel, you will not believe me. They have just given us a car for Medjugorje! And the name of the donor is ...Joseph! He lives in Lourdes and loves the Blessed Virgin tremendously. He had promised Her to give Her his car, a 305 Peugeot in good condition, but he did not know how to do it. When he found out that I was leaving for Medjugorje with you and that we needed a car, his heart immediately lighted up. He understood that the Blessed Virgin wanted his car for Medjugorje.

We have the exact time to prepare the registration documents in your name and the insurance, and I am coming with the car to leave with you..."

And do you know what? The letter was dated November 9, the day when the novena began. But Saint Joseph had kept his promise and slowed the post office. He is a man who is very faithful to agreements. The answer for me had been scheduled for Friday the 18...

And this 305 always bears today "it has made the war" and has enormously rendered services to the glory of the Gospa.

A good tip to remember from this story: if you need something for the service of the Gospa, ask Saint Joseph and tell him: "This is not for me; it is for your spouse, the Virgin Mary. She needs it for her plans of peace." For Her he always comes through!

Private fax to Geneviève, May 2, 1992

Dear Geneviève,

Tell Slavko that we are mobilizing all the angels of Medjugorje for his speeches in Paris!

Private fax to Gildas, May 2, 1992

Dear Gildas,[1]

Be alert, in the midst of all these efforts to help Medjugorje, never to forget that it is only through prayer and fasting that the war is going to end.

In the mailings, do not send anything without including the messages of the Gospa. And if, because of all this extra work, you see that you no longer have time to pray, it is better to stop in order to keep prayer because otherwise it would be a trap and a loss of blessings for all. You know, our role is not to replace the media. Here, for example, I could quickly become a journalist; there is an abundance of material to exploit. But I have another call. (Sometimes it is "very hard" because I am full of ideas for super reports, as by chance...)

[1] Gildas was very active and efficient for the secretariat of "The Children of Medjugorje.

News from Medjugorje, May 4, 1992

Dear Children of Medjugorje and all of you who work with the Gospa,

Praised be Jesus! Always Jesus and Mary!

We are surprised to see that some mothers have returned with their children to the village. The living conditions for the refugees are so harsh that they still prefer to live in their homes here in spite of the insecurity. The big problem for these families is the lack of food, closed and empty stores, closed factories, no income... Anguish increases. We call on all those who are in a position to organize a truck of supplies to do it. These private efforts permit covering the places which are not being served by more official organizations like Caritas. We will soon give you the different addresses where you can send your gifts to support these efforts. The trucks which are already ready can serve Siroki-Brijeg and Medjugorje; from there, convoys leave for isolated villages. Let us pray so that everything is well organized in the peace of the Gospa and love.

At the time of this writing, the war is still raging around Medjugorje. Mostar knows no respite; from here we can count each shell. Even the Blue Helmets have a difficult time moving about. The access routes are almost all cut off and the population can no longer leave the city. Many houses have been destroyed. Yesterday evening Ljubuski was heavily attacked; the Blue Helmets left this morning to see the bodies of children who have been killed to make their report. Some shells fall on Citluk; two cars are in flames. The village of Medjugorje itself remains completely intact up till now. Some beautiful bonds of solidarity are being established. Pray especially for our soldiers. They now have a routine of 24 hours at the front for three or four days at home. They have taken up again mechanized farming and work in the fields but they are constantly on the lookout. We gave several of them the messages of the Gospa in Croatian. The results? Many claim them and state that they have never read them! They know in their hearts that their Queen alone will show them how to win the true victory. A Franciscan from the parish gets into a military uniform every day to go and look for them at the front but with the merciful heart of Jesus in order to speak to them and to hear their confession. Was the war necessary for them to accomplish this extraordinary stake which rests on Medjugorje and the graces poured out here for the world??

Dear brothers and sisters, your prayers are the wall against which Satan will be crushed. Thank you for persevering in this prayer in these days of suffering. That is certain: the Gospa will win the most beautiful of victories. Thanks to all the love that she will have gleaned from your hearts.

You are her dear children; she trusts you!
Peace be with you!

News from Medjugorje, May 7, 1992, 2:00 p.m.

Dear Children of Medjugorje and all of you beloved of the Gospa,

It is a month now since the first bombs fell on our region of Herzegovina and since Medjugorje, the most visited village in the world, was transformed into desolation... It has been a month since its church was shut down, since its mountains were deserted, since its confessionals are empty, since its loud-speakers are silent, since two thirds of its population have been evacuated... Apparently Satan has won a beautiful victory in this place which he hates more than any other but this is the time for believers to meditate on Jesus on the cross at length and with love. Did the enemy thought of annihilating it? It only caused the release of an unbelievable out-pouring of glory and the opening of eternal sources of life where it believed to have fatally wounded its victims. At this moment Medjugorje and all the Croatian people live their sorrowful mysteries in the expectation of their glorious mysteries. The Gospa is looking for true believers to believe with her in the Resurrection and in this long Croatian Good Friday. She has not left Medjugorje a single day. She appears there to Ivan and Vicka; she prays with them and with all the people stating to what extent our suffering is also hers. Her face is sorrowful; she does not say anything except the means for stopping the war. She carries the whole future of Medjugorje and her immense role for the salvation of humanity in her heart.

She prepares invisibly the great sign she has promised to give on Apparition Hill for believers as well as unbelievers. She has her plan and she will accomplish it. Our function is to hasten this accomplishment by drawing nearer and nearer to her heart thus leaving the least time possible for Satan to destroy.

Dear Gospa, we love you, but increase our love because it is infinitely that we want to love you!

News from Medjugorje, May 8, 1992, 9:00 a.m.

The news from here is not getting better, on the contrary. The city of Mostar is bombed each day; the dead are not counted anymore. The large shopping center has been destroyed and yesterday evening the residence of the bishop was bombed and completely burned from the inside. He himself as well as his priests are alive. The inhabitants take refuge in the cellars because there are some artillery positions even in the city. Do the Serbs want to make of Mostar a new Vukovar? They are on the way! Hunger is already here. Although very dangerous, the only access route permits the forwarding of food but many of the hungry cannot come to the distribution places because of the anguish which is prevalent.

Siroki-Brijeg, Citluk, Dobro Selo and other hot points continue to be the targets with wounded and dead each day. Father Jozo is very active in the help given to his flock who have taken refuge in Makarska, visiting them often. Thanks to the Italian Caritas and other foreign contributions, provisions were given them. In some hotels for refugees, they pray 3 or 4 hours a day to respond to the call of the Gospa. Father Orec, former pastor of Medjugorje, is also very active in Makarska among the refugees of Medjugorje and Citluk. All your trucks will be welcomed be it at Makarska (where the milk for the babies is badly lacking, especially for two-year-olds, as well as little pots for the babies), or at Medjugorje where we have centralized the help to many of the villages, or at Siroki-Brijeg.

Medjugorje remains a preserved place of prayer! We do not need to concentrate a long time to cry out our intercession to God. The shells, planes, explosions, sirens... unceasingly remind us that some men, women and children are about to die and that the Destroyer is doing his deadly work. Yesterday, during the Mass in the cellar of the presbytery, we heard a sound: "the planes, the planes!" Actually we heard them very near as well as the bombs they were sending. The priest had to stop and did not know whether he should to continue. What should he do? It was a raid on Mostar and the area of the Neretva. Many were crying and there was a reason to. This morning it began again.

11:30 in our cellar

Two planes passed by; some rockets fell some kilometers from the church... I will update you tomorrow. Thank you for your prayer and your love. We know in Whom we have placed our trust!

♡ and peace!

News from Medjugorje, May 9, 1992

Dear Children of Medjugorje and all of you beloved of the Gospa,

Our message of yesterday had hardly left for Croatia to be faxed there when Medjugorje received the first missiles in its history... Toward one o'clock p.m. 6 rockets actually fell on the area of Sivric which many French know for having stayed there. We were able to go to the place after the event and confirm the facts with our eyes; no human victims, thanks to our Lord! Two homes had their front damaged and some others their windows broken. A cow[2] was killed. One of the rockets fell hundred and fifty meters from the bridge and 400 meters from the church. Two fell near the access road to Medjugorje where one turns toward Sivric and another fell 50 meters from the home of our friend Josip S., from the rear. Everyone says: "The Queen of Peace has protected us." Everyone says also that the Serbs were aiming at the church. It is true that they have missed it but only by little.

The same day, May 8, our entire region was seriously attacked: Grude, Siroki-Brijeg, Ljubuski, Citluk... And there were some human victims.

Ivan has left for a few days in Italy. That is it for the local news. Let us continue to turn together toward the mother of our lives. Let us help her with all our hearts to protect our dear Medjugorje which she cherishes like the pupil of her eyes. May everyone be in peace; nothing will happen here that is not for her greatest glory and that of her Son Jesus. May their names be praised, blessed, sung and exalted, now and for all eternity!

♡ to every one!

---

[2] To tell the whole truth, a cow, a dog and a chicken were killed.

Private fax to Gildas, May 9, 1992

(Gildas, a brother of the Community in France is responsible for transmitting my faxes. One day, I learned from him

that he spent some hours calling everywhere to try to find out the truth about an important rumor concerning Medjugorje.)

Dear Gildas,

... In a similar case, wait peacefully for my news in prayer. If something important happens in Medjugorje, do not worry. I will rush to the post office at Vrgorac, first thing on the next day in order to send it to you. Do not forget that you are not a journalist but a man of prayer. That is very important. I strongly recommend it to you so that you may preserve the spirit of the "Children of Medjugorje" well. Read the messages again; you will see what pleases the Blessed Virgin. She is not waiting for words. She likes for us to be detached with respect to the current state of the news. She herself does not give any except the means to stop the war, and with that we have the essential. We are not charged by her to systematically spread everything that is taking place. No. When you receive a fax, you disseminate it and when you do not receive any, you remain in peace and you wait. If they ask you something, you answer calmly that you do not know. You well understand that if I insist, it is that this slippery slope would venture to move you away from the ♡ of the Gospa by doing too much. And that would serve her plans; that would be the last straw! I say this to you with great trust, of course...

News from Medjugorje, May 11, 1992, 12:15 p.m.

Dear Children of Medjugorje, dear brothers and sisters in Christ,

Praised be Jesus!

Father Jozo is in England for a few days.

Here we had... almost an apparition! Actually the visionary Marija came to spend 48 hours in Medjugorje before returning to Italy with her sister Milka. She left us this morning. We were able to interview her; the substance of her words seemed nearly the same as the interviews with Vicka, Ivan and Father Jozo. Marija was in excellent spirits in spite of her bad health.

Yesterday Sunday new bombings over Medjugorje, fortunately without any damage. At 12:30 p.m. some rockets fell on the territory of Bijakovici near the none-asphalted route which leads to the Neretva, to the left of Podbrdo. We were there, everything fell far from the homes on a rocky terrain covered with little thorns at approximately 300 meters from the hamlet. Did the Serbian pilot release his deadly devices willingly on a side to spare the Oasis of the Mother of God or did he think that some Croatian soldiers were hidden there?

At 5:15 p.m. during Mass new bombardment; this time over the area of Krstine, one kilometer from the church. Then over the area of Tromedja, three hundred meters from the new gasoline pump (its owner had larded it with miraculous medals!). We are more and more prudent, and spend more time in the cellar...

Forgive me for this rather rapid fax! We remain very, very united with each of you in the burning heart of the Gospa.

♡ and peace!

Private fax to Cyrille, May 11, 1992

Dear Cyrille,[3]

Guess what? Marija came to the house yesterday evening; a beautiful surprise from the Gospa? We took advantage of it to ask her many questions about the situation. We were able to record her on tape (in Italian) and she said a few words for you in Croatian.

She is in very high spirits but she still suffers from this mysterious virus which she caught in South America. A very rare virus; no doctor knows exactly what it is. She has suffered a lot these last months in Italy; standing on her feet was for her a torture. She said to God: "I want to carry my cross well until Easter, but at Easter you will pastor me!" She is better now; she can walk but the actual treatment is uncertain. I hope that this story will end quickly.

She came 48 hours to see her parents. Things are difficult for them at their advanced age. You imagine the house without this little bee which Marija is, always polishing this or that...

---

[3] Cyrille Auboyneau spent seven years in Medjugorje. He served as translator for the visionaries. Author of the book "Words from Heaven", Edition des Beatitudes.

For us her trip has been a true ray from the sun, from the Gospa. Although we know her well, her presence always communicates to us a warmth from heaven; we needed it! She always creates an uproar with Maurice; she is always delighted like a kid! Later he said with pride: "Can you imagine, I received some punches from a visionary!"
And your conferences? I hope that you will continue more than ever. In these times when the "visible Medjugorje" is in the catacombs, it is extremely important that the "Medjugorje in dispersion" strongly raise its voice in the world!

Interview with Marija

Sister Emmanuel: -"Marija, how do you see this war?

Marija: -In Medjugorje we do not experience the war as such; we must go to the front to experience it. Of course we hear bombs but from another side I experience peace for it seems to me that this situation helps us to approach God more and to place our hope in Him alone.

Sister Emmanuel: - Are you surprised of this war in Bosnia Herzegovina?

Marija: -I had been expecting it for some time. Because here there are more problems than in Croatia due to the mixture of populations. But when one arrives here from abroad, one experiences a great peace. It is truly the Oasis of Peace. I think that the Gospa will not permit it to be destroyed.

Each day, I have the habit of recommending this whole situation to the Gospa. It is not a human war but a really satanical one. Going to the homes to massacre the old people or to cut off the hands of children... that is a terrible thing! A human being who has a heart, a family, cannot do such a thing. They are all under drugs; and thus they are not aware of what they are doing. A war will never be able to be forgotten especially this war which is satanical and maintained by people who are possessed by Satan, by very important politicians; for example, masonry is very strong in this war.

With us there is a proverb "Satan never sleeps..."

Sister Emmanuel: - With us, he doesn't sleep either.

Marija: - It is true! But I have high hopes.

Sister Emmanuel: - And how is the family able to bear all this? Your brothers are at the front...

Marija: - Yes. They have to go there. But for many of them, there is something positive in this experience. Each time that they commit the smallest sin, they go to confession. They say to themselves: "If we die, we will be in the grace of God!"

Marija smiles on remembering her brothers...

Marija: The old people who have already lived wars like my mother and my father are very nervous. At night they almost do not sleep. All the memories come back: the Second World War, all the horrors... they pray.

They tell us: "For us the most important thing is that your children be safe. We are old; we have already lived. We do not want to move from here." They want to stay here, die here, doing the things they are used to in their daily lives...

Sister Emmanuel: - Does the Blessed Virgin appear to you in a special way during this war?

Marija: - Yes, her countenance is serious, concerned. But she always gives us hope when she asks us to pray and to fast. I am sure that if we listen to her attentively nothing will happen. What is happening now, I accept as a little punishment, but I accept it specially as a sign so that we may wake up...

Sister Emmanuel: - Why do you speak of "punishment"?

Marija: - Because I think that we did not respond to the messages of the Gospa. And even now, unfortunately, we do not follow this message enough where she tells us "take the rosary in your hands as a sign to Satan that you belong to me. The rosary is the most powerful weapon against Satan."

Sister Emmanuel: - When you say "we have not responded", are you speaking of the Croats or of the world in general?

Marija: - Especially the Croats. In other respects I compare us a little bit to the Jewish people. We received immense graces but also many sufferings. I have heard many Croats say: "It is not a gift to be a Croat. We had the Turks for centuries; then we had communism, and now Serbian oppression. It is a continuous slavery!:

Sister Emmanuel: - What is the meaning of all that?

Marija: - I think that with Medjugorje, with the messages from the Gospa, with everything that is happening to us, we are taking part in a great struggle, a struggle against communism precisely. When we see Czechoslovakia or Hungary, for example, where communism was extinguished very smoothly, slowly, it seems that here at home the tail of the red dragon (as the Blessed Virgin says at Fatima) is struggling in a peculiar manner. Communism is not finished yet even if China recognized the independence of our republics something which no one expected.

What is certain is that for eleven years the Blessed Virgin has been preparing us for these very difficult times.

Sister Emmanuel: - Are the apparitions the beginning of the "Pentecost of love"?

Marija: - I do not know, but I see that with Medjugorje it constituted a great union. As though the whole world had become one single country. We see it; when the people come here, Medjugorje has already united them. They do not ask each other where they come from because the important thing is to look for God together.

Everyone tells us: "We will return to Medjugorje because here we find a source which helps us to continue, a source which gives us strength. In Italy they say: "We have known Medjugorje and now we suffer with Medjugorje".

Sister Emmanuel: - Before all the prayers and sacrifices people offer for this war, is the Gospa happy or does she expect more?

Marija: - I think that she still wants more. And if she asks for it, it is because she knows that we can give more. We can always do more because the Blessed Virgin wants for all our lives to become prayer. I think that if we put that into practice seriously, we will become saints.

Sister Emmanuel: - Thank you, Marija, for having shared all this with us. One final word about your sickness?

Marija: - Nothing! That gives me a suffering to offer to God, that is all!"

Even if distressed by the war, Marija is for us all a symbol of joy, the joy of heaven which opens up, the joy of intimacy with God. Allow me to present you two glimpses of Marija and heaven.

Marija does not cease from time to time to wink at one or other of her neighbors. At the beginning that bothered a little because no Croatian girl does that. We asked her then:

- Why do you wink?

- It is the Child Jesus who has taught me!

- How is that?

- One Christmas day, the Gospa appeared with Him. He wanted to play with me; then He amused Himself hiding Himself behind the veil of His mother. Then He reappeared as He winked at me. Then He hid Himself again in the veil... as children who play hide-and-seek do. Since then I also wink while thinking about Him.

Once again, three days after Marija's birthday, I asked her:

- Did the Gospa hug you on your birthday?

- Yes, she gave me a kiss on the cheek.

- Where exactly?

Marija then showed me a little spot on her left cheek and added while laughing: "and I did not wash this little circle for two days in order to keep the kiss of the Blessed Virgin!"

(When I told Daniel-Ange that, he cried out: "and then you rushed to hug Marija where the Blessed Virgin had kissed her, of course!

- ... Euh... no!
- But you are nothing!")

Private fax to Geneviève, May 13, 1992

Dear Geneviève,

Okay for your fax. Let us strongly wish that you come to Medjugorje. Along the coast, very possible. In Makarska, take Vrgorac, Ljubuski, no problem; many take this route every day. The Gospa will protect you as she protects us; she has seen others!

Josip is in the front lines near Mostar until Monday with forty men from Medjugorje... your most muscular angels will not be enough!

We are eager to see your good face again; we will tell each other some good stories enjoying a good raki; A little relaxation will do good!

News from Medjugorje, May 15, 1992

Dear Children of Medjugorje, beloved of the Gospa, praised be Jesus!

Your prayers are not in vain. Since the cease-fire of Medjugorje, there is a clear lessening of combat and Medjugorje is peaceful. Some occasional sirens and artillery rounds toward the Neretva. Thank you Lord, for this respite because the last count was hard. In Citluk, the hospital was hit and is unusable; in Mostar the parish church of the Franciscans was completely destroyed also and the convent badly damaged. The one of the Franciscan Sisters completely burned down... were these plans of military strategy? No. They were strategic points for prayer, the service of God and the alleviation of suffering!

Like the other visionaries, Marija is right in remembering that this war is not human but satanic. Only Satan can drive man to cut the hands of a child, to cite only an example.

Many ask: "What does the Gospa say about this war?" Many would love the details of her part over such or such a means of acting on the issue of combats... No, she does not say anything. She prays. She does not speak either of Serbs or Croats or Blue Helmets or of the EEC or of President Bush. She prays in silence as she prayed in the hours of the passion of her Son when she could have increased the steps and supplications to the Jews and the Romans...

No, the silence of her communion of love was stronger, more effective than anything. She shows us there the essence of our journey to follow in order to hasten the victory of love over hatred.

The message of April 25 contained everything: prayer, fasting, consecration to the hearts of Jesus and Mary, the stones of David against the giant Goliath, the only infallible weapons against Satan.

"Beloved, how it would be easy for me to stop the war if more people prayed..." she said in December, 1991.

But there it is; some are still missing! Marija told me Sunday that "the Gospa expected more prayers from us because she knows that we can give more". What she wishes is that our whole life become a prayer and that is holiness. She wants holiness from us; that is why she came to Medjugorje."

And Vicka yesterday: "The Gospa only prays with us; she does not speak to us. And she suffers. We see the sorrow on her face and she experiences great suffering in her heart because of the situation. But she shows some hope."

The suffering of our mother is an admirable mystery. Each wounded in this war, each person in agony at the front, each broken heart, in her entire being she experiences everything as if it were happening to her. When Jesus was on earth, she intimately experienced all His sufferings; she was crucified with Him because of her indescribable love for Him. And now, in the midst of this war, she experiences everything, everything, everything because we are the body of Christ and her children and she loves each one of her children as she loves Jesus no less! She said it.

How would we be able then not to love her more and more, not seek to console her, to pastor her broken heart?

May our prayer be the embrace of our heart with hers; may our prayer be joy of love that you share.

I thank all of you very much in the joy of being with you, together, the child of such a mother. Blessed be she!

"They do not have any more wine..." (May 15, 1992)

As in every week, on Friday, it is Maurice's turn to prepare the table of the Shabbat[4] for the liturgy of the evening. On that day, after Mass, we begin to

---

[4] A basic component of our vocation is to live in great proximity with the people of Israel and that manifests itself among other things by the celebration of the 'Shabbat on Friday evening. Folowing the Jewish people, Mary, Joseph, Jesus, and some

at sing the Canticle of Canticles around the table, then the psalms in Hebrew. On the table have been placed the two breads of Shabbat which we have specially made this morning and also the cup which will be filled with wine, at the moment of the "Kiddoush" (blessing of the wine, then of the bread).

In the middle of Psalm 23 ("the Lord is my shepherd; there is nothing I shall want..."), the entrance door is opened noisily and steps climb the stairs. A man is there; he waits behind the curtain which separates our dining room from the landing. One only hears his breathing and also the crumpling of a plastic sack. Each one asks: "Must we interrupt the liturgy to go see who it is?"

Then an arm appears on the side of the screen, a big hairy arm and everyone holds his breath. The arm has an unusual bottle of red wine. He lays it on the ground. Then the steps turn back; the man is going to go back. I look at Maurice who has suddenly understood everything: a pitcher of wine set on the table (designed to fill the cup) is empty; he completely forgot to fill it. This afternoon, seeing that we did not have any more wine, he said to himself: "I will go to Sivric quickly to get some after Mass!" But he had forgotten. Without knowing it we had begun the Shabbat without wine and the moment of the Kiddoush was going to come...

And here was this man, not knowing anything more about it, bringing us the wine which we needed, exactly at the last moment!

I made a slight signal to Cécile who was only waiting for it in order to go behind the curtain to see who he was. It is our friend Marko who lives at the foot of Krizevac. In order to thank us for the cartons of food which came from France, he brought us some wine from his vineyard, but did not dare to interfere with our prayer... Divine Providence will always astonish us!

Thank you, Lord, and... Shabbat shalom!

Cécile relates...

Christians of the first centuries, we live this magnificent family liturgy around the table; a liturgy which makes us anticipate the Kingdom, the eternal rest in the heart of God.
Here in Medjugorje the Shabbat is enriched in a peculiar dimension. Actually, according to tradition the mistress of the house lights the candles of the Shabbat sunset. Because the Jews know that if sin entered the world through a woman, it is through a woman that the light will return to it. In Nazareth, it is the Blessed Virgin who lit the lamps of the Shabbat. She, the Mother of Light, made flesh. In Medjugorje it is truly with her that I light the candles because here more than elsewhere she gives birth to the light again in the hearts to save our sick generation from darkness and to prepare the coming of her Son in glory. '

Once again, during the war, before the Shabbat, Maurice calls me into the kitchen:

- "Please, taste this wine! Do you think that it is appropriate for the Shabbat? That is all I have.

- Pouah!... But it is vinegar!... What do we do? Do we put it in just the same? What is Emmanuel going to say?

- In any case, we did not have any other", Maurice answered me.

... At the moment of the blessing of the wine, we were waiting for Emmanuel's reaction when she would taste the vinegar. Not only did she not make a grimace on drinking the cup, but when Maurice himself drank from it, his face showed great astonishment. I asked myself what he was hiding. Such was my surprise to confirm, on drinking in my turn, that the wine no longer had the taste of vinegar but that of a delicious wine!... The Lord came once again time to show us His loving tenderness by changing... not water into wine but the vinegar into a Saint-Emilion!

At the end of the liturgy, I explained to Emmanuel:

- "Unbelievable! Before the blessing, the wine had the taste of vinegar. Now, it is delicious!"

She answered me without batting an eyelid:

- "That is normal; it is the Shabbat!"

News from Medjugorje, May 19, 1992

Dear Children of Medjugorje, dear brothers and sisters in Christ,

Praised be Jesus! Always, Jesus and Mary.

A great joy for us yesterday to see our "men of Medjugorje" all safe and sound, among them Vicka's brothers and our friend Josip, return from the front after seven days in the front lines of the side of Mostar where the danger is at its peak. Your angels worked very well; thank you for sending them to us! No wounded, no deaths. They said that it was a miracle with the number of bombs which exploded above their shelters. Josip told me: "You cannot imagine the thousands of Hail Mary's that were prayed! Everybody was praying. It is the Gospa who saved our lives."

Vicka set us a good example during these days. She remained completely cool and joyful even knowing her brothers and her cousins were in the front lines and hearing like we did the explosions of the bombs in their sector... "Why worry and be attached to the radio? No, it is useless! I have the homework; I continue to do it and each day I devote all my attention and my heart to it..."

The Blue Helmets left Bosnia-Herzegovina. The order came from Sarajevo and those from Medjugorje were very disappointed. We too! Under their aegis, five thousand children were able to be evacuated from Mostar just before Major General Peresic (Serbian) declared that no one could leave the city. Many children are still there and risk their lives! Sunday, we were able to follow the air raid on the approaches to Mostar; it was impressive. First of all, we heard the planes flying over us; then the chains of bombs exploding; the noise from the Croatian aerial defense (several planes crashed) and finally we saw the thick black smoke rise from Mostar... Yesterday morning, the very same thing over the villages between Ljubuski and Vrgorac, but the bombs fell on a side. No victims.

Ivan returned Sunday the 17th from Italy. He reminds us that it is important to live what the Blessed Virgin asks in her message of the 25th.

Vicka left for three days with Father Orec to thank the Italians for all their help they sent to the refugees. With her collaboration, we prepare a leaflet addressed from the Croatian people and especially the refugees in order to comfort them again in their trials and to show them how much they can be powerful to stop the war on the side of the Gospa who chose them first (Marija told me: "We, Croats, feel a strong communion with the Jewish people.") This leaflet will contain the last messages, the letter from Vicka, a picture of the Virgin of Tihaljina and some messages of the earlier years when the Blessed Virgin expressed her desire and her plan for Medjugorje. This leaflet will be printed in France and distributed to the families of refugees in their different places of settlement (the coast, Zagreb...). Our goal is to approach these beings who have been torn apart by the war from the heart of their mother who does not cease to cherish them and to call them. "Dear children, I burn with love for you... Abandon your hearts to me!"

Next weekend we expect new trucks bringing provisions. A large part will leave for Bosnia where they do not have anything, through the intermediary of the Franciscans and of some safe men because these villages have become the object of terrible massacres and it is dangerous to go there. Three days ago, some children of thirteen and fourteen years of age were hurled by the tens into the fire near Tuzla, and others mutilated. Hundreds of persons had their throats cut with a knife, especially Muslims, who are very numerous in this region. It is an absolute horror. It seems that the Serbs have a kind of madness of despair, but at the same time, many of them rebel against their leaders and their senseless orders and desert them. May they be the majority and thus cause the rage to destroy to be aborted.

We greet and we thank from the bottom of our hearts all those who were touched by this simple news from Medjugorje (which, to our greatest surprise, leaves for the whole world!), all those who have expressed to us their profound communion, and all those who give us material support. Their gifts serve for the mailings and for the intense dissemination of the news and the messages, for humanitarian trucks, for the help of several families of Medjugorje and, finally, for the leaflets in Croatian for the refugees.

We greet and give thanks from the bottom of our heart to all those who persevere in prayer and who humbly, courageously, live the messages of the Gospa. I am very eager to tell them with the Gospa: "If you knew how much I love you, you would dance with joy!"

The Serbian Army... the slave ship!

Our friend Zeliko (pronounce Gelico) told us that a soldier from the Serbian stronghold which controlled Mount Velez (overhanging Mostar) returned here to the Croats. He is of Muslim origin. He says that up there, many men have the typhus. He was sent by his leader to look for water at the foot of the mountain. He took advantage of it to desert because since he himself had typhus, he was not able to do anymore. The Croats received him and sent him to the hospital in Split. He weighed only forty kilos. He said that every morning in the army, they are made to take a white pastille which is a drug, but he does not know the name of the drug. He says that after that the soldiers act as though they are out of their minds, ready for anything because they no longer weigh the danger.

I hope that experts will be able to clear up the truth concerning the use of drugs by the Federal Army, in order to stop this course of death. It deals in all likelihood with a drug "speed" or amphetamines, but there are others. The goal is none other than to make the soldier "hyper-courageous" to permit him to remain sleeples for a long time, make him lose all notion of danger and to arouse in him the desire, the driving need to fight. A bloody desire capable of giving man an almost superhuman strength during combat but... at what cost, because these drugs are totally suicidal. They already have thousands of deaths to their credit.

Zedenka, Josip's sister, a nurse at Otocac (this village of Croatia coupled with the "Children of Medjugorje") narrates the arrival of the Tchetniks in her village. The Croats had organized their defense to stop them. A first wave of Tchetniks came toward them without taking any precaution against the danger. They ran unprotected toward the village; they cried out like animals while waving their weapons above their heads, and the majority fell under the Croatian bullets. Then a second wave came. They yelled the same way like crazy people while waving their weapons and they trampled over the bodies of the first wave as though they had been mere stones under their feet. They ignored every danger. Several hundreds were thus killed; they were under drugs and... the right dose was there!

That is why many Serbian soldiers crack and desert their ranks. Of course, they are captured; they are given weapons by their army. Those who succeed take refuge in Croatia and they request to be able to call their families in Serbia. Their army in effect does not document any deaths although the Serbian families are in terrible anguish. Evidently they do not want the war...

Since thousands of Serbs have already been killed and it is necessary to follow the mad dreams of Milosevic, young people, sixteen and seventeen years of age, are dragged by force from their family in Serbia in order to go and fight in Bosnia-Herzegovina. Their distress is unspeakable.

Some men from Medjugorje found certain ones attached to their cannon by kinds of chains to their feet. It is necessary to stop them from fleeing when combat is raging! Let us not talk about hunger, sickness, the harshness of camping conditions...

I am a witness to the fact that many inhabitants of Medjugorje pray even more for the Serbs than for their own people because, they say, they are treated worse than beasts. For months they have been far from their homes; they are constantly the object of black-mail: "You are going to the front lines or we will kill you..." The Communist army is without pity. In Medjugorje, I did not attend a single Mass when we did not pray for them. So that the peace of God may triumph over this massacre of bodies and hearts.

The children will overcome hatred

Since the beginning of the war we have been asking the Gospa each day: Make use of us to stop this war; show us in prayer what you expect from us and our presence here.

That day in prayer I became convinced of one sure thing: it is the children who are going to help the Gospa in her plans of peace. She is in need of their innocent little hearts in order to annihilate the inflamed features of the Evil One.

I went up to my room and while I had no imagination, I began to write down on a piece of paper several ideas which are to capture the attention of children and to propose to them to help the Gospa. I spoke about them with the brothers who reacted enthusiastically. Nicky[5] told me: "Wonderful!"

I went immediately to Vicka's house to ask her for her collaboration because we often see each other to exchange information about the war. Before so many atrocities (which she saw more than I on television), we often asked each other what we could do more for peace, besides prayer and fasting. I explained to her then precisely my idea and to my greatest joy she also reacted enthusiastically.

- "That is going to help the Gospa very much", she said to me several times.

We then shared the work; each one would do according to his own grace. After several meetings, everything was finally ready and Vicka told me with her great smile:

- "If you have other ideas like that one for peace, tell them to me; I am ready!"

She promised me to pray to the Blessed Virgin for this project. (To my knowledge, the Blessed Virgin said nothing concerning this project, but Vicka's willingness was to me a positive sign; at least it did not displease her!)

Well, before America there are some little children in the village who are first: rank has its privileges! In fact, I get to the presbytery with the letter from Vicka in Croatian. I meet Father Iko (in charge of catechism) and hand him my papers. He reads them attentively though he is in a hurry. Then I hand him all the first designs. He almost grabs them from my hands. I say to myself "That is it; it does not please him..." I stuttered.

- "Nije dobro?" (Is it not good?)

- "Very good", he said to me "but I barely have the time to make copies for my children in catechism. The class is right now..."

---

[5] Later on he would be in charge of the translation in English.

Monthly message of the Blessed Virgin of May 25, 1992

Dear Children:

Today also, I invite you to prayer so that through prayer you come yet closer to God. I am with you and wish to lead you on the path of salvation which Jesus gives. From day to day, I am closer and closer to you although you are not conscious of it and do not want to admit that you are connected to me in prayer only a little bit. When temptations and problems arise, you say, "O God, O mother, where are you?" And I only wait for you to give me your "Yes" so that I pass it on to Jesus and that He may bestow you with the graces. Therefore, once again, accept my call and begin anew to pray, until prayer becomes joy for you, and then you will discover that God is almighty in your everyday life. I am with you and I wait for you. Thank you for having responded to my call.

News from Medjugorje, May 28, 1992, Ascension of Our Lord

Dear Children of Medjugorje, all of you beloved of the Gospa,

Praised be Jesus Who is with us every day until the end of the world!

For several days the village has been very calm and a glimmer of hope begins to dawn on our men of Medjugorje, because in several places the Croats have been able to regain the terrain which the Communist army had taken; it is a little but it is something. That is very costly in human terms: at Ljubuski, yesterday, even deaths of young people, of seriously wounded. One could read great seriousness on the faces of the young soldiers, eighteen years old; twenty, for sure: "We will never be the same." They matured by ten years within a few weeks. They have another taste of life. They know where the essential is and where to find it; "these passing things the world presents to you" as the Gospa told them... One would have to write a book about them...

Ivanka returned after a week with her children; this can be seen as a good sign. On the other hand, Marija could not return. Father Jozo is now in the United States, in Washington. For three days Ivan has been having his apparition in the cellar before Mass, with the people as in the first years... A great blessing for us; we entrust you, you who cannot come, to the Queen of Peace.

They tell me what the French media are disseminating in France (and else where?); it makes us want to cry. The task of a journalist is to come to the field to see, hear, capture what really happens. In 1940-45, were they informed in the four star headquarters of the Gestapo in Berlin to learn what was happening in the concentration camps?? Why then do they get their information from Belgrade today, in the Serbian Communist Headquarters, with the number one aggressors of this war, to describe what is going on in the Croatian and Muslim zones of Bosnia-Herzegovina as well as with the Serbian people, their own people, who have no more trust and are rebelling? Journalists, why are you going backwards on this point? I have some work to suggest to you which will allow you to prepare excellent reports on hot topics.

Five questions to journalists: (thank you for delivering them).

* Come to Mostar. (If our friend Nicky has been there three times these days, you can do it too.) Open your eyes, your ears and your cameras and tell us what is happening to hundreds of Croats and Muslims locked up in the large Orthodox Church, without water and without food.

* Mostar: Question the Serbian officers and ask them what crime their own men have committed to be hanged by them on the bridge (and no one dares to remove them).

* Go into the Serbian infirmaries in Bosnia-Herzegovina and take pictures of the blood samples from the Croatian and Muslim prisoners to the last drop, to death for the transfusions of the Federal Army.

* Go and interview the Serbs who have perpetrated the massacres specially in Bosnia and ask them what these famous drugs which they are made to ingest before combat are. There are three kinds of them. Obtain these drugs and prepare a scientific report on their effects of bloody madness.

* Finally, your best paper will be a filmed interview of several pilots responsible for bombing Medjugorje, who have parachuted when their plane was hit, and captured by our Croatian forces. They said that they could not bomb Medjugorje because when they were approaching, they did not see anything. The village had disappeared; a kind of cloud was hiding it from their eyes. We want to know more about it. Dear journalists, find these pilots and tell us everything, everything, everything!

In the great fight against hatred which is especially a spiritual fight, Father Slavko has stated that the parish of Medjugorje decided to live these words of Jesus: "Love your enemies, bless those who hate you; pray for those who persecute you..." in the course of the great novena to the Holy Spirit which begins now. The Gospa had often recommended this novena before Pentecost. Thank you for uniting with your heart for thus the level of love will increase enormously. That is more than necessary. "Through love, dear children, you will do even what seems impossible to you" said the Gospa to us.

She was pierced through by the hatred Satan stirs up more and more in the world. Three days ago Vicka said: "You know, when we see the face of someone who is suffering, we say to ourselves: 'it is going to pass; it will be better tomorrow.' But the Gospa, she has the face of one who is going to begin to cry, and on the following day things are not any better. On the contrary, each day she suffers more."

Each one of us can receive this trust in his heart, in the silence of his communion of love... In these times when Jesus and Mary are looking everywhere for consolers, each one of us can say "Here I am".

Peace and ♡ !

The incense of the enemy

Did the Blessed Virgin appreciate the fax of May 28? I am not sure. The morning after my conscience was heavy with a certain uneasiness; it is not my role to pull up the suspenders of journalists or to use the provocative language of the media to deliver this information. On her part the Blessed Virgin uses all other means in order to "establish justice which bears peace" (Zach. 8,16). The solution to peace is never to put oil into the fire, or to add more to already serious matters.

In other respects, the evil is not centered completely on one side which would be that of "the enemy". On two sides of the front are both saints and demons and in every case of the children of God, my brothers.

Who is for me "the enemy?"

Let us call a spade a spade. I live in a small village; I love my neighbors, the inhabitants of the village, the visionaries, the priests. These people have become my family. In April, war planes flew over us. In May, we were bombed. I know that a whole army has something against our lives, and that it wants to destroy us. I call "enemy" him who wished me evil, him who would be happy to destroy my village, my home, my family and who puts all his power in doing it. In the Gospel when Jesus speaks of the "enemies", those whom we must bless and love, it is about them that He speaks. Objectively, there exists someone who wishes me evil. He is then this enemy I am going to try to love and to bless with all my heart.

In any case the enemy is not he whom I do not love or he whom I wish to do wrong. When we learn that a Serbian plane has crashed near Capljina, I am distressed to see the joy on certain faces, the joy of vengeance. I think of the young Serbian pilot, father of a family, who is about to appear before God, and my whole wish is for him to fall in the embrace of love as quickly as possible. And I weep for his wife and his children who have not wanted this war, and who will never see him.

This attitude of heart is much easier for me than for some Croats because I did not live in these villages which were decimated by the Tchetniks. I did not attend the slow martyrdom of a son or a daughter whose eyes were removed, or of a child who was cut into small pieces before me. Forgiveness then is truly heroic and I know that many Croats live this forgiveness. They do not speak nor do they write about forgiveness; they live it with all their bloody heart. Without knowing it, they have thus become the most powerful instruments of the Gospa for her plans of peace. They precede me by a long shot and I pray to have the grace to be like them some day.

Among the Serbs, I know that there are also saints, people who pray especially among our Orthodox brothers. Politicianss, often directed by badly inspired human beings, greedy for power, that is often the only and sole reason for which we do not oppose each other on the matter. Political indoctrination is an invention of Satan which has provoked millions of deaths with these peoples who had everything to coexist harmoniously.

This Tchetnik who, beyond the Neretva, today fires his cannon to destroy my village; this same man could very well be, in other circumstances, a brother of my community, an intimate friend, a close friend. He has a heart like mine. His first identity is that of a son of God, and I do not want to consider him differently than in that light. My Croatian neighbor who eats at my table, behind whose cannon would he be if he had been born, not in Medjugorje, but in the suburbs of Belgrade?

A little before the war broke out in Bosnia-Herzegovina, the Lord gave me a sign.

Belgrade, January 1992. I had a stopover for a few hours at the airport and I saw an empty table in the bar in order to be able to read and write. I told the Lord: "If You want me to speak to someone, You Yourself make him come to this table. Five minutes passed then I saw a man coming all dressed in black who sat while he smiled at me. I saw by his bearing and his hair that he was a Serbo-Orthodox monk. Since his English was even more lamentable than my Croatian, the conversation took place in "Serbo-Croatian".

- "Do you know them?" I hasten actually to show him the beautiful pictures of the visionaries which appeared in the book of the messages.

- "Yes, I have followed the matter a little at the beginning. But you know, Medjugorje, for us Orthodox..."

- "I know. Podbrdo 1941, the massacres[6] ... But the Gospa had to appear at the same place forty years later."

- "I too believe that the Mother of God is appearing down there. But the Croatians did not listen to her messages. She said: "Be reconciled!" They have not done it. That is why there is war" (in Croatia).

I kept silent because he was partially right, even if the summary was a little hasty. The visionaries themselves know that the message of reconciliation was not taken seriously by the Croatian people.

He spoke to me at great length about his vocation, then about his life at the monastery. He asked me questions about mine and discovered with amazement that Seraphim from Sarov (great Russian Orthodox saint) is a patron saint of our community. A real communion was born between us and the joy of being brother and sister. But his plane was going to leave very soon and he quickly looked for a gift to give me a sign of this fraternal communion. He went through his large bag also black like his robe, and handed me with a radiant smile, a large packet of rose-scented incense, which had come directly from Athens. He could not find better. For several months I had looked for our liturgies it in vain .

Three months later. When we were celebrating our Vespers in Medjugorje, when the burning of the bombs blended with the melody of our chants, we rose to the Lord the perfumes of this incense. Are the planes from Belgrade flying over us? Yes. But in the heart of the enemy, I know that there is also love. And I am happy to pray with him beyond this absurd war. Did our windows shake under these bombings? Yes, of course. But I know that love will conquer because fortunately what rises from the altar with our evening prayer is the incense of the enemy.

[6] Exactly forty years before the apparitions, a band of Croats made a large number of Orthodox perish by hurling them all alive into a very deep natural cavern which they stopped, abandoning them to a very slow agony. This place of massacres is found exactly on the other side of Apparition HIll. These massacres were reprisals of other massacres carried out some time before by the Serbs toward the Croats... The hellish higher bid of hatred!

IV

June 1992: Testimony of love from poor and little

News from Medjugorje, June 1, 1992

Dear Children of Medjugorje, beloved of the Gospa,

Praised be Jesus!

Medjugorje is still very calm; we can still follow with our ears the artillery of our forces which are conducting offensives to drive back the Serbs. Let us pray together for both sides, so that the ones will recover their lands and their villages, and the others may be guarded against despair. You do not imagine the distress of the Serbian soldiers. You have heard the disturbances in Belgrade... May the Immaculate Heart of Mary protect these people against those who lead it to its destruction, against their leaders inspired by Satan, the destroyer.

Marija took advantage of a convoy "Caritas" to come to spend twenty four hours with us. Her health is improving for they have finally found the appropriate medicine. I would like to give to you a part of our conversation:

Sister Emmanuel - "You, the visionaries, always describe to us the Blessed Virgin in her visible appearance, but can you speak to us about her character?

Marija - It is very beautiful!

Sister Emmanuel - Even now?

Marija - The Gospa is very sweet and at the same time decisive; she is strong. It is not a sweetness which lacks strength.

Sister Emmanuel: - Continue to explain to me...

Marija - She is also very sensitive. For example, when one speaks to her about something sorrowful, one sees the suffering on her face."

Here is a little glimpse which will nourish your love for her.

I will end with an event worthy of the Gospels. A family from the village received twelve refugees who lost everything, everything, everything. We know them very well; there are six of them and very close to one another. Before the war they had killed a young cow to eat its meat. Thanks to an electrical generator, they were able to keep the freezer going; this saved the meat. This family had an open table for the poor throughout the day, and the food never lacked! They have then eighteen people at noon and evening without counting extra the poor who were always well received. At each meal they ate meat (they are the only ones in Medjugorje because of the lack of electricity and refrigerators). This family has spent all its money to help the refugees. They say "we still have our home, our sheep, our fields; they do not have anything!"

The other evening, I said to the head of the family:

- Where do you get so much meat? So many people after two months, noon and evening, that is very much! Did someone give you another cow?

- No, Sister, it is always the same cow. I do not understand; I wanted to remove pieces from the freezer! it never diminishes. Thus I also give to other families!..."

When I entered the community, several times I had the opportunity to see with my own eyes the multiplication of food. The Lord thus multiplied by the thousands (at the time a closer resemblance to Ars) chicken thighs, loaves of bread, small boat-shaped, chocolate pastry. Prayer with the heart is very powerful, the Gospa tells us.

This family is beautiful; it did not know that the Lord was going to multiply and they were ready to learn themselves about hunger in order to give to all those who did not have anything! How Divine Providence would not have cracked before such hearts? I give thanks with you for this beautiful sign of the sweetness of God in Medjugorje, in these times when men are plunged into absolute horror.

"Blessed are the eyes which see what you see!"

Grace and Peace to all of you.

Private fax to Milona, June 2, 1992

Dear Milona,

Thank you very much for your few words brought by Nicky. We are happy that you work so much for Medjugorje in Munich, but we seriously miss you here! We are doing well; it is necessary to say that it is less difficult for the village than at the beginning of the war. Fewer planes, fewer alarms... And several French friends came to bring trucks with supplies. They spent two or three days with us; that was good for us... (...)

I express to you again my love and my deep communion with the ♡ of the Gospa.

Some toothpaste?

Cécile and I often had the impression of "playing the merchant", because at the house all kinds of women and children who asked for food passed by. Our room was transformed into a warehouse and the mothers of families spent each her turn to take there whatever they needed to survive.

We were always struck by the modesty of their requests. These people lived in such poverty; managed with nothing - a simple soup a day in some families - that before such a display of provisions, they did not dare ask for almost anything.

We had announced the hours of distribution on our door in order to reserve time for prayer. But Croats and discipline... those are two things! Some came specifically outside of the schedule so as not to be seen by anyone. They would say to us: "Do not tell anyone that I came!" Because they experience a kind of shame to come begging for food.

To receive them was for us a true joy. Beyond the joy of offering them with what to survive, we continuously received learning on their part. Thus the good heart of Sofia who, with her husband, had received fifteen refugees among whom were eight children, and these children had already broken practically everything at her home...

- "What the children break, is nothing in comparison to what the Tchetniks have destroyed among us", she said calmly.

Sometimes we held back our laughter with difficulty, and I often found Cécile in a corner of the room with her back turned, her shoulders shaken in a significant way, and I had to quickly flee into another room in order not to risk being annoying to the person whom we were serving and who, without knowing it, had "left a good one". Cécile was champion in communicating the crazy laughter and the tragic environment of the war was curiously a favorable round for this nervous safety valve which is laughter.

One day, a poor woman among the poor came looking for things for her family. She had never seen powdered milk, much less in a tube. We explained to her as we could the doses with the clear impression of "changing her mind". Then, I suggested to her a tube of tooth paste. Then she looks at me without any enthusiasm. I said to myself that my outlay was a little stingy and suddenly I recommended to her two or three. Her face became gloomier... I looked at her and in a flash I understood. She had never used a brush for her teeth in her life, and today... she has only one tooth left!

News from Medjugorje, June 7, 1992, Pentecost Day

Dear Children of Medjugorje,

Welcome to the Holy Spirit prevalent in our hearts on this day!

This morning, about five 5:00 a.m., all of Medjugorje was awakened surprisingly by the violent roar from cannons and then it continued. Very important battles were raging just on the other side of the mountain, around Capljina, decisive battles for the population and our villages here in Herzegovina.

Please pray intensely for our Croatian units so that they may be protected and that they fight without hatred, and for the Serbian units, so that they pull back without destroying anything in their way. Medjugorje cannot be invaded because the Serbian Army is very weakened in this area, but the Croatian soldiers suggested to us not to go away too far from our homes, because things can fall on us from heaven which will really not be tongues of fire...!

Yesterday, the church of Dobro Selo (15 kilometers) was pierced through by a shell. Before yesterday, eight shells near Citluk. No victims. Medjugorje is always preserved. On the contrary, Mostar has been severely pounded and Sarajevo lives a real nightmare. The pictures of yesterday, shown on television, seemed to have come out of a horror film. In Bosnia, killings, mutilations, massacres and tortures continue, and more famine.

Some truck loads of supplies, carried through "Italians Caritas" and by our dear French friends helped to nourish these populations a little...

After Belgium, Father Jozo nas been in France for several days. I have learned that he will visit our Community of the Beatitudes tomorrow! Thank you, Lord, for the gift! Here, Vicka and Ivan continue to have their apparitions. The parish Masses are always in the cellar of the presbytery, with a continuous increase of the faithful and... a similar increase in heat!

For some time the Blessed Virgin has put in my heart an urgent request to help realize her plan of peace: to make the least of her children pray, for the prayer of small children is all powerful to the heart of God. With Vicka's aid, we are preparing something important in that sense. It is a large task (and our means, here, are ridiculous; no telephone, no photocopier...). Thank you for sending us your angels to help us during the seven days which are coming. Peace and ♡!

Vukovar 1992

It was the last days of Vukovar when the Serbian army succeeded in razing the city.

A young Croatian soldier still tried to defend some houses; he was without an illusion. He was killed with his whole unit.

His body was found in the debris, and in his pocket, a paper:

"I know that we are all going to die because we are the last to fight here and the enemy is advancing toward us. A bomb has just exploded in front of me. I was an unbeliever but I have just had an extraordinary experience. I have seen a great light and God was in this light. I saw Him in the midst of bombs and my heart overflowed with joy. I am dying believing in God; I know now that there is someone up there Who is waiting for me and Who love me."

Private fax to Pascal, June 11, 1992

Dear Pascal[1],

For two weeks I have been in the beautiful event which the Gospa has shown me in prayer. You will see the number "Special Children" which will come out soon. But it is international; I stir, then, with the whole world without telephone, without fax, without electricity...

My telephone is now in Citluk, my fax in Croatia (seventy kilometers of

[1]. My brother in Rouen.

mountain terrain; welcome to walks) and Jesus in my ♡ !

Pray so that we may have one more brother and sister. We are extremely touched by all your prayers and different forms of help since the beginning of the war.

Ten billion "thank you's" and ♡ !

Your good sister, Em!

News from Medjugorje, June 12, 1992

Dear Children of Medjugorje,

Praised be Jesus!

Yesterday, until late at night, the noise from the cannons made our doors and our windows vibrate. The Croatian offensive to drive back the Serbian army continues to struggle with full force. The city of Capljina has been liberated. But before retreating, the Tchetniks burned down a large number of houses after having pillaged them. The thick smoke which rose from the city was seen in Medjugorje. The Serbs withdrew near Mostar from where they can still attack us. The order was given to them yesterday evening by their leader to destroy the bridges; they did it immediately so that four bridges were destroyed. There remains only the old bridge where only the pedestrians can cross... The city has been cut into two!

In spite of everything a certain hope rises again in the hearts of the inhabitants of Medjugorje and around, because they have been able to recapture the villages beyond the Neretva, like Stolac, from where the army of the enemy had pillaged them for two months.

Our task now is to pray for the Croatian soldiers who can have the temptation to return evil for evil, massacre for massacre. Their leader Shimun Tomas told them from the beginning: "Do not destroy any Serbian Orthodox Church[2] or any public place. He who does it will go to prison." No Orthodox church in the region was destroyed, thanks to the Lord! They are beautiful with their magnificent icons... But this army truly needs our prayers because there are

---

[2] Two days later I learned that the large Orthodox Church in Mostar had been partially destroyed by an explosion.
Someone told me:

- "It is the 'Paraga' who caused the strike." (Paraga is a Slovene Croat who draws more and more Croatians into his party, the Croatian Party of the Right (of the life). His ambition is to regain the first territories of Croatia which some centuries ago extended

among them men from Vukovar, or from other places in Croatia, and what they have seen with their eyes goes beyond everything that one can imagine. It is holiness that we ask for them; not to massacre the assassins of their families.

Father Slavko has returned. As far as we are concerned, life continues without water, without electricity, without telephone, without... without... this or that, but there is one thing that we do not lack: the joy of belonging to the Lord and to work for the Gospa! And we are truly filled with that, thanks also to your prayers. Thank you with all our heart!

Grace and peace with you!

Private fax to Florence, June 14, 1992

Dear Florence,

... Your food continues to make people happy. Pray very much for Nicky who is going to Sarajevo on Monday and who has loaded his trunk with your preserves... He is going to try to take out one of his Croatian friends from this closed hell, on a path for him....

---

to the Drina River. He is perceived as an extremist.)
Others told me:
- "It is the Muslims who caused the munitions to explode in order to take vengeance for having been held there as hostages."
Still others:
- "It is the Tchetniks who conducted the strike before withdrawing into the mountains so that the Croatians are not able to dispose of their munitions." (In fact, the church was serving as a munitions' depot to the Federal Army, and they had an enormous quantity of them there.)
Where is the truth? There I lower my arms; I know that I will never know it.

News from Medjugorje, June 15, 1992

Dear Children of Medjugorje,

Praised be Jesus! The war continues in Bosnia-Herzegovina especially in the regions near Serbia where the horror is at its peak. The situation in Sarajevo is so dramatic that the city seems to be destroying itself inwardly because of the factions and splinter factions which kill each other. Famine, settlement of accounts, tortures, anguish, impossibility to leave because of the encirclement... The silent victims of the hatred of Satan call us and implore us!

Vicka told me yesterday that the Blessed Virgin did not show any improvement, any relief in the sorrow of her countenance although the situation of many villages is better in Herzegovina.

What does she see? What does she anticipate?

As I was telling you last week, we have already started with Vicka an important operation of help to aid the Gospa in her plans of peace. And that thanks to the smallest of her children, thanks to these small ♡ innocents whose prayer is so powerful to the ♡ of God. In fact, Vicka has written a letter to the children of America and to all the children of the world to suggest to them to help the Blessed Virgin to stop the war. For that, they are invited to enter into "the army of the Gospa", an army whose only two weapons are prayer with the ♡ and sacrifice with the ♡ . In order to motivate them to the maximum, we made eight designs to be colored, adapted to their young age, on which they would be able to report their prayers and their sacrifices and these designs would be sent to Vicka who will offer them to the Queen of Peace. The adults would have an important role to play in the preparation of the ♡ of these children for this operation of help, especially in explaining to them to what extent their prayer is powerful. "Through prayer, you obtain everything" the Gospa tells us.

Vicka shows great enthusiasm for this operation: "It will be of great help for the Gospa, she says, and it is certain that she will reward us!" Thousands of American children are already working on their designs... With yours, they will give the Blessed Virgin the power to make great, great miracles of love!

Vicka thanks you with all her ♡ and I also thank you.

Grace and Peace!

One must take the rough with the smooth

This operation for the children allowed me to experience a grace appropriate to the events in Bethlehem: the joy in poverty.

In fact, the call made by Vicka and I had to touch the five continents and it was with absolutely no material means that we had had to work.

* No typewriter; everything had to be done by hand.
* No photocopier... It is the hand of Cécile which duplicated the texts.
* No artist.
* No possibility of getting a copyright to protect the text.
* No telephone at home; I had to go ten kilometers from Medjugorje where a telephone worked at certain hours, but only in one way (I could call, but no one could call me from abroad). In Medjugorje I could sometimes use the line at the presbytery because I had the green light from the Franciscans, but since it was the connection to a military line, the calls should last only five minutes in order not to block the calls indispensable to the army...
* No fax in Medjugorje. I had to go to Vrgorac, thirty eight kilometers from the mountain opposite the place where the telephone was and go through five or six road blocks on the way. There, I could send some faxes and receive some from abroad.
* Rationed gasoline...

Joy, joy! One day while I was dialling for the twentieth time a number on the telephone which was "dead", I said to the Lord in order to provoke Him; You know, those who work for Satan, he makes available to them an ultra-sophisticated equipment or material. Four-star offices, trilingual secretaries, working computers, telephones and faxes of the latest model, international networks on satellites... and all that to create darkness galore. And I who want to work for you, look into "what state am I wandering"... You ask me to have these papers sent to several countries and I do not even have a single telephone available to me, nor even an adequate felttip pen to make the contour of the designs...

I had to make sure that the Lord did not allow Himself to be at all impressed by my words, because in the course of the following days, He did nothing to better the situation. Then I said to myself: "It is His Will which is taking place thus." Actually, all things considered, it brought me closer to Joseph and Mary in the mystery of Jesus' birth. They had to give birth to the grace of graces for the world and that, in almost non existing material conditions. I understood then that for God, true success was not in the quality of the performance but in the growth of our hearts. His humility and His poverty. For it alone will remain for all eternity. Of course, we must work hard but never forget that true fruitfulness comes from Him and not from our human effectiveness.

That does not prevent humor between us, because I continue from time to time, to make amusing remarks to Him concerning His confusing way of proceeding with His friends...

News from Medjugorje, June 19, 1992

Dear Children of Medjugorje,

Praised be Jesus!

The eleventh anniversary of the apparitions is approaching, and today, the Gospa gave us a gift which elated our hearts: the evening Mass will be celebrated no longer in the cellar but in the church, reopened yesterday at nightfall. Wind blew, all were in need of it! To find the church again is to find the pulse of life for the whole village. The priests recommended being extremely prudent, to maintain the cellars accessible and to obey the sirens. Actually, even if the villages around were "liberated", the village could still be the target of an air raid and even of certain cannons which have remained pointed at us from a mountain still held by the Serbian army. Numerous pilgrims were announced for the anniversary; they were welcomed in spite of the material conditions which will be very precarious. It was recommended to each one to bring his food (the stores are empty and the restaurants closed) and to prepare himself interiorly for these many annoyances, great or small, which often go on a par with the greatest graces!

To all those very numerous ones who would like to come but are not able, thank you for taking this day of June 25 to honor the Gospa in a very special manner in communion with Medjugorje. Thus it is together, closely united in one intense prayer, that we approach her heart and receive her blessing of peace for the world. These concrete steps of prayer are more than ever necessary; the Gospa is looking for her children, her "supporters" more than ever in these very critical times. For Medjugorje is not so much a land of pilgrimage to safeguard as a spiritual victory to bear to the heart of the world; that of love that saves souls against the hatred which loses both bodies and souls. And this war... oh, how it is raging these days!

History books will relate to you better than I do the horrible massacres of this week. I am not speaking to you of Bosnia, of Sarajevo especially which has become worse than Lebanon, but from regions close to us. Ten minutes by car, entire villages burned down; we drove along the Neretva, several houses were still in flames. We entered Mostar; it is the second Vukovar, especially the old city. Near the airport, before yesterday, a gigantic blood bath: the vengeance of the Croats against several hundreds of Serbian soldiers who had tortured to death many near by populations. All of that is brought to our doors: fifteen, twenty, twenty five minutes by car, at this moment. From both sides, hatred has been aggravated. That is why, more than ever let us unite our hearts and our voices so that Satan falls paralysed by our prayer and can act no longer. Satan who is afraid of a four-year-old-child in prayer!

I rejoice that many children have already received the letter from Vicka with the pictures. Thank you for encouraging them to be little good fighters on the side of the Gospa... They have the power to stop the war!

Marija returned from Italy for the anniversary. In Rome recently she had a private conversation with our beloved Pope John Paul, II. The nature of this conversation must remain private; I can only say to what extent the pope is in communion with Medjugorje, rejoicing in its graces and suffering its difficulties. We have in him a true father, nothing astonishing on the part of this son of predilection of the Blessed Virgin!

Grace, peace and courage to each of you.

But Jesus said to them: "give them yourselves to eat"
(Matthew IX, 16)

Vinko is a good friend of Vicka who was miraculously cured of his eyes through a grace of the Gospa. His daughter lives at the foot of Krizevac but he himself lives with his wife in the surroundings of Split where crowds of refugees have crowded now fleeing their villages in flames, abandoning their homes, lands, work and very often husbands or children, in order to seek shelter.

Vinko is not very rich. Everything just to make ends meet for his family. But his heart overflows with love and before the distress of certain refugees, he decided to be the good Samaritan. So much and so well that he is with twenty two refugees in his home. To give them lodging is not really a problem; in the evening they put some blankets on the ground and they sleep, some close to others in the manner of Croatian families. But... he must feed them! There are some children, adolescents: no need to make them fast.

Vinko is a simple, practical man, a rustic, a child of the Gospa and he knows that she said one day: "Dear children, let love always be your only means."

He takes then the food destined for the survival of his family, and he shares it with twenty two refugees. It is the fruit of his little piece of land at this time of the year; some potatoes and beans. Such was his surprise then to see that the potatoes multiplied themselves! He gave, he gave... and there were always some.

In February he planted ten kilos of potatoes. He was expecting thirty five kilos, forty five maximum (that is what the earth produces here). For on the day that he told us that, June 22, he had already harvested five hundred and thirty kilos and it was not over. He spoke with emotion, and tears of joy, of tenderness, flowed down his emaciated cheeks, emaciated and chiseled by the sun. And he added: for the beans it was the same thing! He has something else to say. He hesitates; he becomes frightened... He ends by stating:

- "You know... for money... it was also the same thing. I had a little money in my pocket; I gave it to them to buy some basic little things. Later I still had some; I gave them... and each day, I do not know how, money comes to me. And that has been going on since they came to the house!"

Tears prevented him from saying more, but we had all understood: "There is no God like our God!"

Private fax to Vincent, June 22, 1992

Dear Vincent,

We are living a kind of vertigo; at the approach of the anniversary, pilgrims begin to arrive. The bombs have calmed down (or almost!) and Medjugorje regains its former face. In two days, one goes from one world to the other; we cannot believe it! We inhale at last; that makes us feel good. Water returned this morning; the electricity, yesterday... It is a beautiful life!...

News from Medjugorje, June 23, 1992

Dear Children of Medjugorje,

Praised be Jesus! Always Jesus and Mary.

Joy and sorrow blended, such is the feeling which embraces our hearts on this day at the approach of the eleventh anniversary.

A joy to see that the front has moved back forty kilometers from Medjugorje.

A joy of our church again opened after seventy five days of catacombs; a joy to find the children playing on the street; joy to receive the first pilgrims; joy to listen to the loudspeakers resounding with the litanies of the Blessed Virgin instead of artillery crackling its shells...

Sorrow to feel the tears of the Blessed Virgin weeping over this country traumatized by hatred while she came to give reconciliation and peace. How many years will it take to cure so many wounds, how many Pentecosts of love to permit God to draw good from evil?

Yesterday was the worst day for Sarajevo. A hundred people murdered. Settlement of accounts, absurd or desperate gestures. "Satan makes fun of your souls, the Gospa had said, and I cannot help you because you are far from my heart!"

Yesterday in Mostar, a Franciscan told me in front of his destroyed church: "Jesus was in the tabernacle; He burned with all the rest. And eight days ago, I performed the funeral ceremonies for my brother. They had cut him into pieces. I had to gather every piece to reconstruct the body before the funeral ceremony. His wife and six children are on the coast as refugees; they cannot return because their home has burned down. Sister, pray so that I do not become crazy. That I may remain calm, that I may remain calm!"

The worst thing in this war is what has been done to the children, to the innocent. But on this point I will keep silent. It is they precisely, the children and those who resemble them, who console the Blessed Virgin and her Son. Tomorrow, we will give over to Vicka the first pictures from the children, and she will offer them to the Gospa for the anniversary when she appears in her splendid robe of gold. These pictures come from America. An American told us yesterday: "I do not have any small children, only a daughter thirty years old. I showed her the number "Special-Children" and she told me: "Mama, I am thirty years old but I am your child. It is I who will make the pictures for the Blessed Virgin!" What beautiful example of a good heart, for all those who do not have children to whom to give the pictures! Each one is the child of someone!

To the American, Canadian and European children, I would like to send a huge "thank you" and also tell them a little story in order to show them how much the love of one single heart can work miracles. A man from Medjugorje was very poor, and because of the war he had almost nothing to eat. Only a few kilos of potatoes. And there came some refugees still poorer than he. He decided to receive them in his home and to give them the few potatoes in his possession. Seeing his good heart, other refugees also came to ask him. At the end of three days, his meager quantity should have disappeared. Well, it did not! Not only did it not disappear, the more he gave his potatoes, the more his stock increased! And thanks to it, he was able to feed many poor. With ten kilos at the outset, he found himself with five hundred and thirty kilos of potatoes. The same miracle occurred with his beans which he has distributed without counting them. He was so moved before this gift of God that he cried when he told us that. And that reminds me of a word from the Gospa: "Through love, dear children, you will do even what to you seems impossible!" Then continue your pictures; it is your love which will stop the war!

In this love, I express to you my communion.

Monthly message of the Blessed Virgin of June 25, 1992

Eleventh Anniversary of Mary's Apparitions in Medjugorje

Dear Children: Today, I am happy despite there still being some sadness in my heart for all those who began to take this path and then abandoned it. My presence here is, therefore, to lead you on a new path, the path of salvation. Thus, I call you day after day to conversion. But, if you do not pray you cannot say you are converting. I pray for you and intercede before God for peace: first, for peace in your heart, then around you so that God may be your peace. Thank you for having responded to my call.

(The Blessed Virgin gave all the people present her special blessing.)

News from Medjugorje, June 28, 1992

Dear Children of Medjugorje,

Praised be Jesus!

On the occasion of the eleventh anniversary, we find again the usual face of our Medjugorje; that was very good! Only the important number of soldiers in uniform, the military trucks and the explosion of some shells have shown the foreign pilgrims (almost two thousand) that the country was still at war. We hope that this renewal of the pilgrimages will continue and will intensify. We greet the courage of all those who shared in the "March of Peace", eleven kilometers on foot between Humac and Medjugorje, under a beating sun.

In her joy, the Gospa invited all of us to the mountain the evening of the 24th for the apparition. She blessed us and Ivan addressed these words to the crowd that was present: "I bring you peace, dear children, carry it to others. You are those who are going to carry peace to the world." She was wearing her beautiful dress of gold.

On the 25th, in the course of the apparition, Vicka offered her the first pictures of children as a gift for the anniversary. The Blessed Virgin showed her joy; she blessed them as well as the children who had prepared them. Vicka is waiting for the others impatiently!

This same day, Ivanka had her annual apparition in her home. She told us that the Gospa had a grave face. In the course of the apparition, Ivanka raised her hands and held those of the Blessed Virgin. The latter said: "I ask you to conquer Satan. The weapons to conquer him are fasting and prayer. Pray for peace, because Satan wants to destroy the little that which you have."

Marija received the monthly message, and she saw the Blessed Virgin give every one her "Special Blessing". This blessing is very unusual, and it has a particular meaning; it carries a special grace (see "Words from Heaven", p.114).

Father Jozo had returned after a long stay outside of these frontiers. In Rome, in the course of a private meeting with the Holy Father, the latter said to him: "It is necessary to protect Medjugorje." The Holy Father seemed to regard this place of prayer very highly; this is what was most important in the conversation.

The Archbishop of Split, Monsignor Franic, celebrated the vigil Mass of the anniversary. During his homily he recalled the strongest messages of the Gospa, and how each one of us could work with her for peace. The warmth of his words was so intense that the crowd began to applaud in its enthusiasm!

News from the front in Herzegovina? It is still thirty kilometers from

Medjugorje. The Croats are trying to neutralize the strong Serbian places near Stolac, also near Mostar. Many pilgrims have been able to see in Mostar the serious damage due to the bombings. But the city is again off-limits; the mayor asked the refugees not to return there because yesterday six shells still fell on the city. On the day of the anniversary, it was the route to Mostar which was also the target of shells. New houses were burning.

Let us persevere faithfully in prayer with the ♡ !

I greet all of you with the immense joy of having been able to find many of you again, and for having seen at what point the Lord has maintained us united (and will keep us united still) during these difficult months of conflict.

Grace, peace and ♡ !

Father Jozo meets John Paul II.

All kinds of testimonies circulate in the church with respect to the personal and private opinion of Pope John Paul II in connection with to Medjugorje. Testimonies of bishops and priests, to whom the Holy Father has advised to come pray in Medjugorje, for example. But it is often difficult to put one's hand on one of these bishops or these priests. I was also very happy to be able to interview Father Jozo personally following his meeting with John Paul II. Here is what he wrote to me:

"My unforgettable meeting with our Pope took place on June 17, 1992 at 11:30. So many friends of Medjugorje had prepared this meeting! I had to accomplish my mission of peace with the general of my order and with the Pope. The Pope had been informed of my mission and the general of my order also. I had already made a brief report to them on my mission of peace and of my meetings with different politicians. Since I had the papers in my hands, I also decided to give the Pope the image of the Blessed Virgin (of Tihaljina) with the messages. He was surrounded by some cardinals and priests. I took his hand and kissed it. He told me "good morning", and with love, he listened to me introduce myself:

- "Holy Father, I am Father Jozo from Medjugorje. At the end of my mission, I want to leave you this report with the image of the Blessed Virgin and her messages."

The Pope answered me:

- "Medjugorje, I know, I know, Medjugorje... Protect Medjugorje. I am with you. I bless you. Courage, courage, I am with you. Support Medjugorje. Greet them all for me. I bless all of them. I know you are suffering in this war."

He held my hands more and more tightly. I continued telling the Pope about the political situation and the sufferings of our people. Full of sadness, he blessed me again while he held my hands tightly. I thanked him for everything that he had done for us, for the Croats and for the independence of our country."

1- Anti-aircraft gun near the church of Medjugorje

2- Bridge at Capljina after the bombings

3 & 4 Homes destroyed in Mostar

5 - Church of the Franciscans at Mostar.

6 - Public garden in Mostar transformed into a cemetery.

7 - Ivan during the apparition of the Blessed Virgin in the cellar of the Franciscans (May 1992). Behind the window, boards and sand bags.

8 - The brothers and sisters of the Community of the Beatitudes in Medjugorje (from left to right: Brother Bernard, Brother Maurice, Sister Emmanuel and Cécile).

V

July 1992:
To hope against all hope

The candles of death

A year earlier...

A village of Croatia like so many others. Serbs and Croats have been living there together for centuries. Night has just fallen. Some children are playing; some adolescents, strolling. They have brought the animals back and they are not so eager to go to bed. It is so good, so sweet on this evening of spring.

In a Croatian family, two children are whispering delightfully. They are plotting without the knowledge of their parents. This evening, in fact, they observed an unusual detail at their neighbor's house: a candle was placed behind the window of the kitchen. What is funny is that it is not only at the neighbor's but also in several homes of the street.

- "Surely it is a new game; we are going to do the same!"

Our little cherubims were waiting for everyone to be asleep and stealthily slip into the kitchen. They placed a candle as evidence before the window...

- "There it is, we have done as our neighbors!"

Very early in the morning, the father woke up and went out. Astonishment: a large packet was placed on the sidewalk immediately in front of his door. Not only before his, actually the same packet was before several doors on the street... Odd! He examined closely...

- "And what are those candles behind the windows?" Each time more and more bizarre! He opens the packets: some weapons, some munitions!

That is it! He understood: only the windows of the Serbian homes have a candle and each of these homes has its package in front of the door. Not the others. Easy to conclude: the Serbians are preparing for the war; they are arming the Serbian families.

- "The children, is it you who have placed a candle in front of the window of the kitchen?

- Oh... Ben... we would like to play also...

- Very well, children, very, very well!"

Without knowing it, they had foiled the secret sign of recognition of the Serbian homes; those who should receive the weapons that night.

News from Medjugorje, July 3, 1992

Dear Children of Medjugorje,

Praised be Jesus!

Before leaving Medjugorje for ten days, some news:

The local press greeted with great admiration and enthusiasm the "March of Peace", which took place on June 24 by a large number of pilgrims on the initiative of our German brothers. Eleven kilometers under the hot June sun... A beautiful gift for the Gospa!.

Marija has indeed fully recovered her health and does not stop receiving friends and pilgrims during these days, consoling each one with her high spirits and joy. She left Medjugorje yesterday to go to Scotland with Father Slavko and teach in a spiritual encounter youth group.

In the north and east of Mostar, the front is slowly but surely moving back. The Croatian soldiers from Croatia, who have come to help those from Bosnia-Herzegovina, have returned to their homes. This makes things more difficult before the Serbian strongholds. Atrocities of all kinds continue in Bosnia; thank you for not weakening in prayer and sacrifice for thousands of lives. The fate of thousands of souls depend on it. With spiritual weapons, we will fight so that hatred may be uprooted from hearts.

In the pictures offered by the children to the Gospa on June 25, some little Americans had added to them distressing words of love, while explaining the sacrifices they had made: "I did not suck my thumb... I did not drink any soda today... I did not cry..." There you have our "first lines" against the Destroyer. We are truly eager to follow them; they make the heart of the Gospa melt.

I would like to encourage the intense renewal of the pilgrimages to Medjugorje. Thus I echo the sentiments of the Franciscans. Actually, by land, by boat (Port of Split) or by plane (Split), there is no problem. And all those who come are caught up by the intensity of peace which reigns in the village. Welcome!

On the evening of June 29, the Blessed Virgin invited us again to the mountain for the apparition with Ivan. Accompanied by three angels, she said: "Dear children, in a special way this evening, I want to invite you to abandon yourselves completely to me. Leave all your problems, all your difficulties with me... I ask you especially to renew my messages in your lives. Pray, dear children, for in these times I need your prayers..."

Dear Gospa, we are happy to make this exchange with you. We will give you our sufferings and our cares; you are going to take care of them better than we and on our part we will take care of your intentions, with your plans... It will thus be a double victory!

Peace and ♡ !

News from Medjugorje, July 15, 1992

Dear Children of Medjugorje,

Praised be Jesus!

A great joy to rediscover Medjugorje after these ten days in France, especially a Medjugorje which is calm and peaceful, where groups of pilgrims begin to succeed one another. Many persons asked me: Can we return? Here is the response: not only can you return, but it is highly desirable that you return because this way you are sure to make the heart of the Blessed Virgin glad. She is waiting for you, to help you pray better for peace, to better make peace in your hearts. On the mountain in the evening, she often expressed her joy before the pilgrims: "Dear children, I am happy to see you this evening in such a great number!"

Marija is in Italy after her stay in Scotland, but Vicka assures the welcome of groups with all the enthusiasm you know in her. Ivan is also here and has invited us these last weeks to pray on the mountain in the evening. The last two requests from the Gospa were "Pray for Peace!" After the United States, Jelena spent the summer with her family.

The route of the coast is free up to 100%, even at Zadar, and planes assure flights to Split. Come in crowds!

At the heart of this very grave situation, the Gospa has visibly wanted to take care of these free zones, these protected corridors, in order to keep her promise to her "Oasis of Peace". Her plan is really for peace to come from there, from Medjugorje. Coming here to draw peace from this fountain and living the messages is indeed stronger than signing treaties of peace, which are always violated.

In Bosnia there are concentration camps where thousands of people are held captives. For months people have not been able to go there. They will probably say after the war: "It existed and we did not know it!" Sarajevo is one thing, but the media does not say anything about these villages which have been destroyed, razed, leveled with a bulldozer, then covered up with earth as though they had never existed. In all of Europe, the obsession of a single man: "to purify the earth" (as others had the obsession to "purify the race") was enough to break the life of several peoples, simply because he had the power! And we allowed it! Of course this famous land does not have petroleum, but the true reason is somewhere else.

These last months the Gospa has well clarified for us what it is that is destroying us. We are still far from the heart of God, for God alone is our peace. Her task is to bring us closer. Oh, let us allow her to eliminate the distance that still separates us from her Son to plunge into this abyss of sweetness and tenderness which is her heart and thus hasten the hour of peace. Let us participate in the sufferings of the true Orthodox believers from Serbia and beg the Father to give these people a shepherd according to their heart!

May grace and peace of God be over you!

News from Medjugorje, July 22, 1992

Dear Children of Medjugorje,

Praised be Jesus!

It is still sorrowful joy that grips our hearts in these days. The country is as if broken in two: on the one hand a large zone of peace in Herzegovina allowing the Croats to return to a normal life, also allowing Medjugorje to welcome its pilgrims; on the other hand, an important zone of conflicts in Bosnia where the tragic surpasses the imagination. For reasons which escape me, the Serbians almost exclusively blame the Muslims. The current operation consists in "cleansing" one after the other the cities where Serbs and Muslims used to live together. It is thus that three days ago, the Serbs gave this ultimatum to the Muslims of the city of Bihac (pronounced Bihatch) in Bosnia:

"You have forty eight hours to leave the city." This city had thirty five thousand inhabitants. Tens of thousands of Muslims have been on the road, without shelter, without food for twenty four hours... That is only one example among others of these last days. Europe does not act. Humanitarian aid is absent from these very dangerous zones.

What should we do? I often hear say: "It is a cancer in the heart of Europe; it is going to degenerate in a catastrophe for all countries." No! That is not fatality; on the contrary, our prayer is full of hope. In the first years, the Gospa said this to Jelena: "The purposes on the fatality of catastrophes come from false prophets. They say: 'On such a day, at such an hour there will be a catastrophe'." I have always said: "The chastisement will take place if the world is not converted. Call men to conversion. Everything depends on your conversion."

And let us remember this promise made at Fatima: "My Immaculate heart will triumph."

In the course of a recent evening apparition, the Blessed Virgin asked that we pray very especially for Pope John-Paul II and for priests.

Let us remain united in prayer, but a prayer full of the joy of Christ and imbued with thanksgiving. (That is a sure way of dismantling Satan's plans!)

Grace and peace!

Monthly message of the Blessed Virgin of July 25, 1992

"Dear Children!

Today again, I invite all of you to prayer, a joyful prayer, so that in these sad days, none of you feels sadness in prayer, but a joyful meeting with God, your Creator. Pray, little children, so that you can be closer to me and feel through prayer what I desire from you. I am with you, and everyday I bless you with my motherly blessing, so that the Lord will bestow you with abundance of His grace for your daily life. Thank God for the gift of my being with you, because I am telling you, this is a great grace. Thank you for having responded to my call."

News from Medjugorje, July 29, 1992

Dear Children of Medjugorje,

Praised be Jesus!

Medjugorje is preparing itself to receive the youth of the world whom the Gospa has invited for the third festival. Marija, having returned from Italy for the 25, will encourage meetings with these young people, as well as Vicka and Ivan.

Marija was telling us yesterday: "This war is a cross for us, and a sign for you. Why a sign? Because deep divisions which have caused the war here also exist in your countries. If we had listened to the message of reconciliation, we would not be in war now. There is the sign for you."

Jelena, the visionary of the heart, is resting before leaving for the United States to study. Each day, she continues receiveing internal locutions in prayer. How does the Gospa lead her? Jelena answers that the locutions are more and more intense and deep, leading to the presence of God specially in the Eucharist. Jelena astounds the pilgrims by the supernatural peace which emanates from her.

Unanimously Franciscans and visionaries invite all those who would still hesitate to come on a pilgrimage. Vicka adds: "Let them not fear; they can decide in their ♡, because there are no problems. Everything is free from now on at home!" Having been questioned on the countenance of the Blessed Virgin these days, Vicka confided that it expresses at the same time sorrow and hope.

The front is always twenty kilometers away as the crow flies, from Mostar which still receives from five to ten shells a day, although the refugees have not been able to return to their homes yet.

The news from Bosnia leaves us in a state of shock. An example among others: in the village of Gorazde, some small children were hurled from the height of bridges into the river. For that the Gospa gives us an admirable response by inviting us to find joy in our God-Creator. He alone, in prayer, can make us understand and taste the greatness and the beauty of the gift of life. Giving thanks for this gift, practicing joy, that is what will conquer inwardly the terrible scorn of live, expressed as much by the massacre of the innocents in our clinics as well as by acts of war. Medjugorje is an important place of cure for the love of life; we pray there each month for that. How many mothers, fathers, doctors, and young people have cried their sins there against life, in the arms of the Mother of Life and have found again peace of the heart in the great mercy of Jesus.

Thank you, dear Gospa, for revealing to our ♡ how to conquer the bridges of Gorazde like the tables of abortions, like the

despair before life which threatens so many children. Thank you for taking us under your maternal care which is constantly leaping with joy!

Peace!

VI

August, 1992: Shout from the roof tops what takes place in secret...

News from Medjugorje, August 5, 1992

Dear Children of Medjugorje,

Praised be Jesus!

The Youth Festival was at its peak; they were fewer youngsters this year but it was very intense. They were able to have longer conversations with the visionaries, and these first-hand witnesses, so near, so simple, touched them deeply. Yesterday, long prayer for peace in a village completely destroyed. They were able to touch the fruits of hatred with their finger and the vital urgency of the message of reconciliation for the world became evident. They will never forget the faces of those poor who have lost everything!

At the time of an apparition to Ivan, the Blessed Virgin addressed a very urgent message to the young people, answering in few words the terrible feeling of emotional and human insecurity which is often theirs before life: "Dear children, I call you to decide for God in the course of these days. You, the youth, put God in the first place of your lives, and thus, you will be able to have a sure way with you. I ask you to pray for my intentions of peace."

Today, August 5, to celebrate the 2008 birthday of the Blessed Virgin, Vicka will offer her an enormous package of pictures from children.

Now here is some information which must be disseminated everywhere, for human lives are at stake.

We knew the existence of concentration camps in Bosnia which were held by the Serbs. No one knew what was going on there. But there were some prisoners who were finally able to escape and one among them, a relative of a visionary, told us everything. We have then the account of a eye witness whose escape goes back a few days.

It is about the city of Doboj. Since May 7, 1992, the Serbs have transformed it into a vast concentration camp, with today between ten and eleven thousand prisoners, men, women and children, Croats and Muslims up to this date. The men were completely separated from their families; they do very hard work and they are struck each day. They live in temporary shacks or underground, in the mines where they are made to work. Many die from hunger because they have only a shabby potato a day and a little water. Their wives have stayed at home and they must check in twice a day. They are the objects of brutality especially in the sexual domain.

Since the Serbians do not want to hold prisoners, a systematic extermination has begun. Each day, a hundred people are massacred, both men and women as well as children. They cut their throats with a knife, often after having made them suffer tortures which our friend described for us but which I am not inclined to specifically state. The anguish is at its peak; the Serbs have forewarned the prisoners that it was a matter of "ethnic cleansing" and that all the non Serbs would end up being liquidated. (It is a logic very close to that of Nazism). The city is completely surrounded; it is situated in a region of Bosnia (Manjaca) between Banja Luka and Tuzla where neither the Red Cross nor the forces of the United Nations could penetrate; they were stopped before. For months then it has been a reign of terror where an entire people has been made to be exterminated without the world knowing it. The few who escaped owe their salvation to the Serbs who betrayed their army in leading our friends secretly out of the camp, on condition that they pay 1000 German marks per person. The risk was enormous for them and several among them were taken and executed before succeeding. And then now, who among the prisoners can have 1000 German marks in his pocket?!

The Serbs are scared to death that the matter of these camps be made known. It is necessary for us then to cry from the roof tops what is going on in secret in order to be able to dismantle it before is too late. All the prisoners are condemned to death; the extermination is in process, inexorably, and each day counts. The Croats beg us to do something; we, foreign countries, because they themselves cannot do anything.

It is astonishing to know that inertia of political Europe, this same Europe which has made so many films and written so many books on the horror of camps. To allow this cancer to develop in Bosnia Herzegovina is the opposite of eradicating it as soon as possible, is not to expose one to see rise the fatal metastases in all of Europe. Hatred is above all a spiritual reality which quickly breaks the frontiers.

It is necessary for a well known and a very spiritually strong personality, for example, a popular writer, a bishop (Catholic or Orthodox), a prominent man, a courageous woman of the calibre of Esther and Judith... to have the courage to come to the place with a highly influenced escort to deal with the Serbs and to demand the liberation of the prisoners. It is two hours from Paris... and some "Marines" were sent to Kuwait!

Thank you for having been on your knees for a long time in prayer; and for those who are able, to move heaven and earth because "whatever you do for the least of mine, you do it for me", Jesus said.

The whole parish of Medjugorje prays with you.

Grace and peace!

The Gospa in the corridors of French Channel 3 (FR3), August 5, 1992

Yesterday evening, August 4, Milona returned to the house and told me:

- "A man came to the parish; he has his family in Doboj, in a concentration camp. He was crying. He begs us to do something."

Then he told me the details of life in the camp. My blood just turned. I still hear the accounts from my father when I was little. He had spent three years in the Nazi camps. With the Doboj, the similarity is striking.

We have to act quickly. With Milona's help, I write out three faxes to notify Paris.

On the following morning, August 5, we were looking for our witness, but the phone betrayed us for such was still the situation in Medjugorje. We could easily call New York or Jerusalem but not the neighboring villages! We had to go to his home by car.

I plagued him with questions. For me it was the day of news; it felt all right, in a few hours his testimony will have gone around the world. The results could hardly be waited; I received a fax from Geneviève B. who, upset by the news from Doboj, set up with me a telephone conversation by radio Notre-Dame (Paris) this afternoon.

Our witness agreed to speak on the radio; Milona translated it. We were cut off ten times, but ten times we repeated our act in order to get to the end of the report.

At the end of the broadcast, Geneviève told me:

- "Some journalists from French Channel 3 will be at my place in half an hour. Call; they want to record you. They said that it was very important."

French Channel 3... Wow! I cannot stop but have a moment of emotion and fear; provided I do not say any stupidities, that I will not put my foot in my mouth which will bring down everything!

But it was August 5; the Gospa will help me because today is her birthday. She will breathe the right words to me.

The Evil One joined in and tried to stop everything by blocking out the lines. In Paris the television team began to be discouraged: "We came for nothing; she is not going to call!"

Finally the connection was established. It was more than seventeen hours. Thanks to the Gospa, my voice was clear, without mistakes. The journalists were delighted and signaled to Geneviève that it was super. 5 for 5. (She said it to me later).

The editing was urgently carried out in the studios of French Channel 3 and that very evening, at prime time viewing, millions of French, Belgians and Swiss could learn what was going in Bosnia, learn the horror of the camps. For four minutes, they saw the church of Medjugorje on the screen; my picture was also seen at this time.

This testimony was effectively carried out throughout the world and aroused an immense offensive of prayer.

On the following morning I received this fax from Lucien, a Swiss friend: "For her 2008th birthday, the Blessed Virgin became pleased; why not? To be frank she really spoiled herself: a long film clip on French Channel 3. No more, no less. With prime time viewing, with a view of Medjugorje, the picture of Sister Emmanuel, Geneviève and everything, everything... It was necessary to do it! That did not go unnoticed. Bravo!"

Yes, she herself could do it and in record time. If I had wanted to have a picture of Medjugorje appear on television, if I had tried to prepare a broadcast to touch the public, it would have been necessary for me to do months of work, processes, crazy money and the results would have left something to be desired.

But she, as if enjoying it, she she took over the broadcast for four minutes! Happy birthday, dear Gospa!

News from Medjugorje, August 12, 1992

Dear Children of Medjugorje,

Praised be Jesus! Always Jesus and Mary!

Vicka has left for a few days in Switzerland for a routine medical check-up. The pilgrims are more and more numerous; that is good. They did not listen to the completely false rumors according to which it would be dangerous to come to Medjugorje. Well, just the contrary! It would be dangerous for our security to everyone, to abandon this Oasis of Peace the Blessed Virgin has specially preserved!

These last days, in the course of the apparitions on the mountain, the Blessed Virgin has told us several times: «Dear children, continue praying for peace.» When she asks for it, it is always first of all to pray for peace in our ♡, then peace in our families and only then, peace in the world. «If you pray for peace in the world and you do not have peace in your own ♡, then this prayer will not be worth as much,» she says.

Thanks to all those who extensively disseminated the last News concerning the concentration camps and extermination in Bosnia. This subject was on all television and radio stations these last times and we are filled with hope that these important places of horror will be dismantled even if in the higher realms of «Europe», some still refuse to intervene to stop this genocide. We have just learned that Jewish minorities are also being held in this region of Doboj. Are we going to open new «Museums of the Holocaust» while there is still time today to stop the infernal machine?

In our world which moves in darkness, «prayer is the only means to save humanity», the Blessed Virgin told us. Then we call on all believers who trust in the living and only God, to pray intensely for their brothers condemned to an atrocious death. Our heavenly Father has a rescue plan for them. It is our prayer for all which will permit the instruments He has chosen, to recognize each other and to enter into action to accomplish it. Without prayer, nothing will take place, except vain agitation!

I recommend, more particularly to my Catholic brothers, to join in a prayer of adoration in the course of nine days between the 13 and the 21 of August (including providentially the Feast of the Assumption and that of Father Kolbe on August 14) the novena ending on the feast of Mary Queen (August 22). Each one of us is invited to send his guardian angel after one who has been detained or a guardian. Thus the camps will be filled with angels and they will accomplish there miracles in hearts. Each one of us will also ask God that new

«Father Kolbe's» (Auschwitz, 1945), rise in these camps and that they cause the triumph of love to shine in the midst of hatred. Finally, we will ask the united hearts of Jesus and Mary to reign over these camps and to hurry the hour of deliverance and of peace.

In their burning love, I thank all of you.

News from Medjugorje, August 19, 1992

Dear Children of Medjugorje,

Praised be Jesus!

Some good news which is going to give joy to us all. Vicka has just told me that the situation was beginning to improve and that the countenance of the Blessed Virgin showed a little more serenity and joy these last days. She was happy to tell me that because for her that is a sign. The Blessed Virgin actually sees things in the divine light even beyond our human sights. Let us continue to helping her with all our ♡ for her plans of peace!

After her medical check-up in Switzerland, Vicka stated that she was in good health. The incredible energy she uses with the pilgrims confirms it!

Ivanka left for the United States for a month.

On the vigil of the Assumption, the Gospa told us through Ivan on the mountain: «Dear children, I call you to renew the prayer of the rosary in your families. Pray the rosary more and offer this rosary for peace.»

Two days ago the parish began permanent adoration (twenty-four hours a day) of the Blessed Sacrament for the intentions of peace. The initiatives were such that they will change the face of the world, while dissolving the inward evil!

Father Jozo expressed a great sadness before the political attitude of France vis-a-vis his country. Let us pray that governments serve God's plans!

Monsignor Zanic, Bishop of Mostar (who left his house exactly five minutes before its explosion last May) has chosen his successor who will be enthroned next year; Father Ratko Peric. We remember that after an exceptional intervention by Cardinal Ratzinger in 1986, the dossier on Medjugorje was no longer entrusted to the bishop of the place but to a commission of «Yugoslav» bishops. The proceedings of this commission were halted because of the war and the fact that its president, Monsignor Komarica, is a prisoner of the Serbs in Banja Luka. We are without news about him.

An emissary from Pope John-Paul II, Cardinal Etchegaray, has just visited Sarajevo, Mostar and Split. He was very shocked at the destruction he saw. On the other hand, he conversed as well with the worst enemies of Medjugorje as with its best defenders... May truth triumph!

A big thanks for your angels who arrived at Doboj, and thanks to the Lord for all the beautiful fruits of our novena of adoration. Initiatives are beginning slowly but surely, but we cannot say anything yet. (You can tell the Jewish authorities that some Jews are here in these camps of extermination; their effectiveness in the quick rescue operation is no longer to be proved; it is a track..) We remain in union with the escapees. They say that many Croatian prisoners came to Medjugorje in the past. Let us particularly support these well beloved brothers so that their offering may cause the bars of hatred to break.

With all ♡, with all of you in this struggle!

Monthly message from the Blessed Virgin, August 25, 1992

«Dear children!

Today, I wish to tell you that I love you. I love you with my motherly love, and I call upon you to open yourselves completely to me so that through each of you I may be enabled to convert and save the world, where there is much sin and many things that are evil. Therefore, my dear children, open yourselves completely to me so that I may be able to lead you more and more to the marvelous love of God the Creator, who reveals Himself to you day by day. I am on you side and I wish to reveal to you and show you the God who loves you. Thank you for having responded to my call.»

News from Medjugorje, August 26, 1992

Dear Children of Medjugorje,

Praised be Jesus!

All this week, our eyes have been focused on Doboj and the camps in Bosnia, on the invisible through prayer and on the visible through the initiatives of help. Prayer always bears its fruit; on the contrary, the efforts to pierce the unsurmountable have not yet ended; patience! An American television team had prepared some footage but one of them was killed in Sarajevo. They then gave up. A French convoy has made some approaches these last days, but unsuccessfully. They had to turn back before Doboj. We salute their courage. Madam Simone Veil took part in this convoy; she suffered in these camps because of her Jewish origin. We hope that she will not stay there and we thank God who gives her the opportunity to work to save innocent lives.

Our faith is beautiful; through it we know that the prayer of the least among us certainly saves some lives. Let us continue sending our angels and praying for the prisoners given up to extermination, by telling us that we could be in their place, in Doboj, as they could be in ours!

Ivan leaves tomorrow for England with Father Slavko for a few days of witnessing.

Jakov always keeps a very hidden life, like Ivanka and Mirjana. Some French speaking pilgrims succeeded in having an interview with him. When the day came, he recited with them an Our Father, a Rejoice and a Glory be to the Father, then said to them: «It is prayer that is most important. The rest is not that important!» And he left...

The positions at the military front have hardly been manoeuvered in the sector of Mostar. The Serbian cannons placed fifteen kilometers beyond the city still send from there, and from time to time, some shells and from Medjugorje we hear the dull and distant sounds of their explosion. The situation in Medjugorje and surrounding villages is very privileged in this war because the population is exclusively Croatian and does not know then the horror of the ethnic conflicts the mixed cities know.

With respect to Bosnia, Vicka said to me: «It is like a chain of fire of which the villages would be the links. When a village burns, the neighboring village prepares itself to burn also. We do not know how all that will end, but we will persevere in prayer and also in hope because the Gospa shows great hope.»

Dear Gospa, today we open ourselves completely to you as you ask of us (confer message of the 25th). Thank you for bringing our sights toward the marvelous love of our God the Creator; thank you for elevating our ♡ toward the realities of heaven because little by little this way our joy and our peace will melt down the bastions of the Destroyer in the whole world. You are our Queen!

Peace and ♡!

VII
September, 1992: Father, forgive them... for they do not know what they do

News from Medjugorje, September 2, 1992

Dear Children of Medjugorje,

Praised be Jesus!

In spite of enormous difficulties and efforts at diversion on the part of the Serbs, a French humanitarian convoy was able to enter Doboj last Friday. To their great surprise, they found the downtown completely deserted, the stores closed, the church burnt down. Where did the population go? Exodus + extermination + distribution of thousands of inhabitants in three camps in the same city. Of course, these camps remained «strictly forbidden zones». The convoy could not bring them any help, but to have gotten that close was an enormous step to overcome.

It is now clear that European governments will not intervene and that Serbia will continue its «ethnic cleansing» in Bosnia with impunity. Our leaders are not scandalized any longer by the scandal... I am afraid, then, that the barbed wires are returning home!

Since no human aid is possible, we are going to continue sending our invisible aid by sending over to the camps, some «parachutes» loaded with treasures, that is to say, descent en masse of our guardian angels. What can ten thousand angels do in a camp of extermination? For example:

- Facilitate escapes (Acts 12, 6-12)

- Inspire in the executioners a profound distaste for torture
- Protect women from rape
- Multiply food
- Dissipate anguish
- Warn someone of imminent danger beforehand
- Confuse the mind of a leader and make it ineffective
- Help a child find his mother; a husband find his wife
- Free from an evil influence (Tobias 6 and 8)

Let us know that our guardian angel is always very happy with our orders of mission (he hates being unemployed!). He moves about like lightning and can be in several places at the same time. The more we pray, the more he shows his presence. He always acts in the sense of the will of God. Each angel sent to a camp is more than a ton of flour!

With respect to this war, Vicka has some enlightening words:

- «When the Gospa asks us to pray, it is for all men whoever they may be. We must pray for the Serbian people whatever they do against us. If we do not show them that we wish them well and that we pray for them, if we do not set the example of forgiveness and of love, then this war will never stop. The most important thing for us is not to try to avenge ourselves. If we say: «They have done me this evil, they must pay, I will do them the same thing», this war will never end. We must forgive and say: «God, I thank you for what is happening to my people and we pray to you for the Serbs because really they do not know what they do». «May our prayer touch their ♡ so that they understand that this war is leading nowhere.»

The Gospa has chosen us to help her; thank you for being these open ♡ where she will be able more and more «to convert and to save this world where there are so many sins and so many bad things».

Grace and peace!

A way to make peace...

The Bible and Jewish tradition teach us very profoundly about peace, about this «Shalom» that comes from On High and which the world cannot give, this «Shalom» of which Mary is Queen...

Cited in the Talmud of Jerusalem, Rabbi Meir has nothing to envy a disciple of Jesus...

Talmud Yerushalmi Sota 1, 16:

Rabbi Zeriah, the son-in-law of Rabbi Levy, narrates the following story:

The evening of the Shabbat, Rabbi Meir had the custom of giving a discourse in the synagogue of Hamta near Tiberias. There was a woman there who came to listen to him on a regular basis.

One day the speaker prolonged his talk more than usual. The woman, returning to her home, found her lamp extinguished. Her husband asked her: «Where were you?» «I listened to the Rabbi's talk.» He said to her: «I swear that you will not return here unless you spit a rabbi on the face.»

Rabbi Meir lived all this in the Holy Spirit, and he acted as though he had bad eyesight. He said: «Let every woman who knows a prayer against suffering from the eyes come close and say it!»

Then the neighbors of the woman said to her: «There you are, this is the time, you will be able to return to your home. Come close as if you wanted to say a prayer, and spit on his eyes!» She approached the Rabbi who said to her: «Do you know how to speak to one's eyes?» Filled with fear she answered: «No.» He responded: «Then spit seven times in my eyes; that will cure them.» After she had spat, he said to her: «Return to your husband and tell him: «You have told me to spit once; I did it seven times.»

The disciples of the rabbi then said to him: «How is it, rabbi, that you thus humiliate the Torah? Why did you not say anything? If you had said it to us, we would not have allowed this man to do it, and we would have corrected him with rods until he reconciled with his wife.»

The rabbi responded: «Should not the glory of the rabbi be similar to that of the Creator? Because the holy name Adonai which was written in holiness, was, according to the Scriptures (Nb 5, 23), plunged into water to be obliterated in order to establish peace between a man and his wife. Should the honor of Rabbi Meir not endure the same outrage?»

News from Medjugorje, September 9, 1992

Dear Children of Medjugorje,

Praised be Jesus!

The mail service is operational again; you can send again your prayer intentions, which will be submitted to the Blessed Virgin through Vicka or Marija (no checks). Note the address:

Children of Medjugorje

Post Office, 88266 Medjugorje, *Croatia*

(It will not arrive if you write «Bosnia-Herzegovina» because Sarajevo is blockaded).

Many men from Medjugorje have returned after spending ten days at the front, because they are lending a strong hand to a region beyond the Stolac where combat is still raging.

Exceptional assessment of the situation since the beginning of the conflict in April: not a soldier from Medjugorje has been killed, and yet they were often in the front lines! Rare are the soldiers here who do not have an experience to tell where they have lived a miraculous protection. And those who did not believe in the Gospa, all believe in her now. The war has been for them the occasion to experience her tenderness as mother. Your prayers have borne magnificent fruits; that is why it is necessary for us to persevere without relaxing.

Friday on the mountain, the Blessed Virgin told us through Ivan: «Dear children, this evening your mother wants to invite you in a special way to pray for peace. I need your prayers...» That means in her words that she is still «lacking» prayers, that she is waiting for more in order to be able to fully attain her plans of peace.

Many are asking us: «How is this war going to end at last?» It is in our ♡ that it is going to end. As long as holiness will grow there, the flame of ♡ and of unconditional forgiveness will burn very strong in us to go and warm the very cold hearts of those who have not received atheistic communism as food and who are threatened with death if they do not kill...

♡ of Jesus, I trust in You!

Immaculate ♡ of Mary, I know that you will triumph!

News from Medjugorje, September 16, 1992

Dear Children of Medjugorje,

Praised be Jesus for His Glorious Cross!

* Sunday morning, some crowds climbed Mount Krizevac for the Feast of the Holy Cross according to a truly living tradition in this region. Admirable faith of the Croats who came to blend their sufferings and the terrible crosses of this war with the Cross of Jesus. The gravity and the depth of the Slavs are an example for us.

* Ivanka returns from America today with her family.

* The Gospa told Ivan that she would no longer appear for the prayer group for three weeks. In fact, each year, she gives them a «vacation» to allow each one to leave the village for a little while. A true Mother!

* Last Friday, she had asked on the mountain: «persevere in your prayer for peace.»

* We are always without news from three camps in Doboj; the horror remains completely camouflaged. Thank you for all the help sent in an invisible way. If we would only know the fruit of the least impulse of our ♡ ! How many situations of despair it cures!

* On September 14, Father Ratko Peric was ordained bishop at Neum. He replaced Monsignor Zanic as bishop of Mostar. Let us welcome him in our ♡ with love and let us support him with our prayers.

* Mostar is still the target of many shells almost daily. The goal of the Serbs is especially to maintain fear.

* On her part, the Gospa continues keeping peace in our ♡ . Vicka can read great serenity on her face these days. * Yes, Medjugorje is really shining like a magnificent star in the night. Medjugorje is the most remarkable fountain of hope in the midst of our world overwhelmed with evil. We could lower our arms before the fits of rage of the Destroyer, before so many and so many sufferings, blindness, sins, before the crucified innocence among so many children... But the Gospa directs and raises our sights toward the victory of God. She teaches us that she and He have a plan of peace *for every situation however dramatic it may be according to a human point of view.*

The visionary Mirjana received from the Gospa revelations, both the most difficult, one on the role of Satan in our times and at the same time the most sublime on the flow of graces never equaled until now in the history of the world. Without in any way betraying the ten secrets she has already received, she gives testimony of the promises of the Gospa, promises which concern the years we are living:

«When the first secret is fulfilled, the power of Satan will be crushed. That is why he is so aggressive at this time. Satan has had immense power in the course of the twentieth century, a power he had never had before and he will not have any longer in the future...»

«... The first two secrets will be warnings to the world of events which will come before a visible sign is given to humanity. *They will happen during my lifetime.* Ten days before the first and the second secrets, I will forewarn Father Petar. He will fast seven days before announcing them to the world...»

Father Petar is forty-seven years old; Mirjana, twenty-seven. If these things happen during their life time... we all have the possibility to know them also. To know the time when the power of Satan will bend to allow the admirable work of God to appear.

Then... courage to every one! We are at the bitterest part of the cup, but the Gospa counts on our perseverance in trials. Because since she is «the Morning Star», she announces the coming of the day!

Grace, Peace and ♡ !

Satan was crying...

What will the time be like when the power of Satan is crushed? It is a question from many of us, but no one can imagine what the Lord has prepared for the future.

And yet, in the history of Medjugorje, the Gospa has wanted in some way a little «general repetition», or rather she has given us a brief view of what her children will be able to live when the Destroyer is kept powerless. Once upon a time...

Father Tomislav Vlasic narrates[1]:

«On August 4, 1984, I was at a prayer meeting with the groups of Jelena, the inner locutionist. The Gospa had revealed that on the morning after, August 5, she would be two thousand years old. During the prayer, I observed a strange thing: Jelena, who had begun to pray the Our Father, suddenly interrupted herself as if her throat had been prevented from uttering a sound. I saw her struggle, but nothing came out. That lasted a few seconds; then she was able to pray again like the others.

At the end of the meeting, I took her aside to ask her what had happened at the time of the Our Father because I doubted that it was a matter of a simple natural phenomenon. She explained to me then that during the Our Father, Satan prevented her from praying and showed himself to her. She saw him on the ground before her, in great pain, and weeping bitterly. He begged her thus:

- «Ask the Gospa not to bless the world tomorrow!»

Then he disappeared. Jelena did not want to pay much attention to him. She told me that a short time later, the Blessed Virgin in turn showed herself to her, and she was smiling. She spoke to her about Satan and explained the reason for his bitter tears:

- «He knows well what he is asking! He knows that during these days he will not be able to do anything in this place (Medjugorje) because he will be tied. The Almighty has permitted me to bless the world with a solemn blessing.»

This blessing of the Blessed Virgin was... her birthday gift!

Actually on the morning of August 5, the graces flowed like a river. The some seventy priests present heard confessions all day and their stoles were wet with the tears of their penitents. And in the evening, they said:

- «We were blending our own tears with those of the people.»

Those days were filled with peace and the graces were considerable. The people went to confession with great ease. And even some said:

---

[1] Intentions gathered on July 30, 1991 at the time of the retreat preparatory to the Youth Festival.

- «We did not intend to come to Medjugorje; we came to the Adriatic Coast on vacation. But without understanding why, we were strongly driven to come to Medjugorje. We were unable to resist this attraction...»

Those days of astonishing graces had been entirely prepared by the parish, which had prayed and fasted on bread and water for nine days. The last three days, the inhabitants had even stopped their work in the fields in order to devote their time to prayer. There were thousands of conversions in those days. And the Blessed Virgin said to the visionaries:

- «Never in my life have I cried with sorrow as this evening I cry with joy. Thank you!»

Father Tomislav added:

- «It is important to bless so as to destroy every action of Satan. The blessing is the greatest gift given in Medjugorje by the Gospa, greater than the messages. It is the time when she touches us inwardly. There can be several blessings according to the gift God wants to give and according to our response.»

Yes, a brief view... which promises!

News from Medjugorje, September 23, 1992

Dear Children of Medjugorje,

Praised be Jesus!

* Ivan is preparing for a long stay in Canada and in the United States, beginning October 8, while Vicka has well decided not to leave the village.

* The very important displacements of populations provoke dramatic situations for the refugees. In Mostar, for example, it is «the war of the apartments». Actually, a Croatian family who had left their home four months before, returned to its apartment and found it inhabited by fifteen Muslim refugees who did not have where to go... Or in the same building, an apartment has been burned down and not that of the neighbor. Should all go into the apartment intact? Justice and mercy do not always go together and many poor have been driven to despair. But these people have a great ability to absorb suffering and their courage moves us.

* Some French families wish to welcome Croatian children. Father Slavko does not betray his people when he answers this: «It is preferable to help the children and the unprovided families in place, not to expatriate them, because it is here that they will be able to reconstruct their lives best, in the bosom of their people. They will help to revive the country rather than to depopulate it.

I add, on my part, that the local youth is happier than the French youth, less tainted by the virus of materialism and thus of despair. Aid associations enter into place then little by little in order to make some sponsorships.

* On the other hand, it is necessary to encourage private humanitarian aid, dispatched by supply trucks. Father Slavko considers two US dollars a day the minimum cost for a refugee, for a homeless person. Since the country cannot assume this expense, it is then up to us, the children of the Gospa, to place everything in operation to help victims of the war. Winter is going to arrive soon; we need warm clothing especially for the babies and the children, and some basic food like flour, sugar, etc. The organizers of pilgrimages from your countries will be able to provide you with information on the means to use.

I state precisely that whatever is brought to Medjugorje is almost entirely sent to Bosnia, the most famished region. Thus Medjugorje lives its vocation of oasis while becoming a kind of turntable for the forwarding of help to Bosnia. A very warm thanks for the small offering from each one!

* How will the Gospa accomplish her plans of joy in the midst of all this chaos? How does she read the events in the light of God?

Just before the war in Bosnia-Herzegovina, she addressed the priests and the bishops from South America (thus the shepherds of the people) through Marija:

«Pray in order to be able to understand these times.»

The Gospa wants us more than ever intelligent in order to help her and it is through prayer that we will become so, because in it she reveals to us the elements of the divine plan for the world...

With all my ♡, thank you!

Monthly message from the Blessed Virgin of September 25, 1992

«Dear children!

Today also I wish to tell you: I am with you in these restless days when Satan wishes to destroy everything which I and my Son Jesus[2]*, are building up. In a special way he wishes to destroy your souls. He wishes to guide you as far away as possible from Christian life as well as from the commandments, to which the Church is calling you so you may live them. Satan wishes to destroy everything which is holy in you and around you.*

---

[2] In the Croatian language we always say "I and you" or "me and him" and not the opposite as in French.

Therefore, little children, pray, pray, pray in order to be able to comprehend all that God is giving you through my coming.
Thank you for having responded to my call!»

News from Medjugorje, September 30, 1992

Dear Children of Medjugorje,
Praised be Jesus!
* The days of the vintage have arrived; all of Medjugorje leads a busy life in the vineyards. Days of family joy.
* Another joy. Mirjana has returned from Italy with her husband and her daughter Marija after being away more than a year. Except for Jakov, all the visionaries are here with us!
* The testimony of the Serbian pilot who had not been able to bomb Medjugorje is confirmed. This pilot was held prisoner in Ljubuski. A matter to be followed...
* In Bosnia, a large number of women, who are pregnant following rapes, are in a tragic, moral and physical condition. Let us pray so that they choose forgiveness and life.
* Doboj soon liberated? Last week, some buses were authorized to come to look for prisoners who could take refuge in Croatia. Let us ardently pray so that this rescue operation can continue because the recent bombings of Slavonski Brod by the Serbs now block the only possible way of leaving this «exodus»... Prevent walking skeletons from finding refuge?
* There is worse: almost all the prisoners of the camp at Brcko (around two thousand) have just been assassinated.
* A neutral commission of the United Nations, delegated in some camps, has confirmed the horrors already filmed by some «wild videos» snatched in silence by courageous journalists.

On the other hand, winter is approaching, and in these regions of Bosnia, the cold goes down to -20 degrees centigrade. That is to say that there will no longer be another person rescued from here for some months.

If Europe does not intervene as soon as possible, it is signing its suicide. It is saying to itself undoubtedly: «Bosnia-Herzegovina is one bad case of the flu. It will go away. Let us leave nature to act...» No, Europe, it is not a bad case of the flu. It is a cancer. The cancer of hatred and if you remain on your chair to sign papers, it will plunge you completely in its agony.

* Eight days ago, Karlo, Vicka's cousin, said to her:

- «Vicka, remember how you cried when you received your seventh, eighth and ninth secrets, and Marija also? If you say that the Gospa did not mention this war precisely in the secrets, then, what are we waiting for???

- You have just given yourself the answer to your question», Vicka answers him.

- It is not by chance if, in her last message, the Gospa warns us very clearly of the workings of Satan. She is waiting for our prayers and the impetuous river of our love to make the barriers of hatred jump and tip, in the ♡ of her Son, our world so sick but so tenderly loved.

Today I decide for love; I decide for holiness.

Peace and ♡ !

VIII
October/November 1992: with Mary... from darkness to light

The wooden cook stove

Hot and wonderful autumn morning, on this October 1st. While passing on the «street of the visionaries», I saw Marija in the little courtyard of her house, armed with an old knife, her sleeves rolled up, scraping the old family wooden cook stove with all her energy. With the help of a thing which in its time was a broom of straw, she was sweeping the thick coat of soot that watered from its blackness the two little medlars which have tried not to die smothered by the pilgrims for three years. Like the rose bushes from Vicka's patio, they have a sad appearance... provided this soot does not kill them!

Marija is in excellent shape, smiling, gay, spontaneous. She seemed as happy to clean its soot as to deliver «words from heaven» to thirsty hearts of our generation. The same work, remove the soot. Deliver the light. Scour, embellish. The same simplicity.

The conversation rambles over everything and nothing while I keep my white habit at a reasonable distance from the completely black appliance.

«The face of the Gospa? Calm», she said to me. Vicka said the same thing this time; it is encouraging.

Marija's knife made the rounds in every sense in order to finish the most resistant plates of soot. Nevertheless, it immobilizes a lapse of a short minute;

the time for her to share an anxiety with me. In some countries, some «Medjugorje prayer groups» begin to follow all kinds of internal locutions and messages which flourish here or there, especially in the United States. Thus they risk deviating from the central message of the Gospa.

I was surprised by the vehemence of her tone and by the real sadness which she expressed before these interferences. I looked then at this very simple girl, capable of playing like a child sprinkling her friends with the hose from the patio and being at the same time the depositary of the gravest messages given to the world by the Queen of Heaven since she has appeared on earth.

«The parish began to move and I wish to give messages as never before in history, since the beginning of the world» (April 4, 1985).

While Marija takes up her broom in her hand, we get to the war.

- Do you think that it is still going to last a long time?

- In Croatia, no. The situation is easier. But in Bosnia-Herzegovina we are not ready to see the end; some years perhaps...

The large American tee-shirt which covers her frail body is about to pass from rose colored to gray anthracite.

With Marija it is at times difficult to distinguish between her personal conclusions (where she can make a mistake) and what flows from her conversations with the Blessed Virgin. Like all the visionaries, she remains very secretive about her daily and intimate dialogues with the mother of God, and it would be ill-advised to question her on this matter.

Through her the Blessed Virgin gives herself to us in an indirect way. She extends her maternal and kindly presence beyond words. One leaves enriched by it and he does not know how it has happened.

On the other hand, Marija makes us always happy by her solid good sense, a good sense in every trial. In the oddest or most complicated situations, she is able to utter a very simple word which deflates the balloon, and relieves our burdened brains from their false questions.

An anecdote from last winter comes to mind.

In January, Marija was in Dublin. One evening, Pat Kenny, a star of Irish television, interviewed Marija at the time of a public meeting which was transmitted all the screens. As usual, Marija spoke with great simplicity about the grace given to her of seeing the Blessed Virgin each day. She explained the principal messages and described the Blessed Virgin just as she appeared to her; a living person whose love is indescribable. The public was hanging in suspense at her words.

Then the journalist, wanting to make a nice bit of scandal (to each his trade!):

- «Marija, all of this, is it not in your head?»

Then very calmly, Marija got up without saying anything, followed by the cameras and she stopped before the journalist. She grabbed him by his shoulders with her bare hands and shook him vehemently.

- «And that, is it not in my head?

That evening, the Gospa was adopted by millions of Irish...

News from Medjugorje, October 15, 1992

Dear Children of Medjugorje,

Praised be Jesus!

* As anticipated, Ivan left Medjugorje for some weeks of witnessing in North America. We are going to miss the evening prayers on the mountain with him! On October 2, the Gospa had given us through him a very important message:

«Dear children, this evening also your Mother wishes to invite you, especially at this time, to pray. At this moment Satan wants to act through little, little things, dear children. That is why, pray! These times, Satan is strong and he also desires to divert my peace plan. He wishes to destroy it.»

What are these «little things» the Blessed Virgin speaks of? Only prayer with the heart will be able to illuminate in our spirits these little flashing lights which will forewarn us of the snares of the enemy in all the little details of our days.

* The situation in central Bosnia is going from bad to worse; the positions are hardening. There are hundreds of dead each day, one or two hours from home. It is hallucinating. Thanks for continuing the humanitarian convoys, at least for those whom we can reach. For the hungry and frozen prisoners, only our prayers and our sacrifices will strongly help them.

* It is a great joy to have Mirjana with us again. Every second day of the month, the Gospa comes to pray with her for unbelievers; often she appears to her as before. Then Mirjana prays in a special way for unbelievers, with special prayers the Gospa has taught her. She confided to us:

«The unbelievers are lucky to have such a mother who loves them with so much love, with so much care. Never does she complain, never does she say: «Enough! I am unable to do anymore». But she always hopes with gentleness and patience. Like a mother, she is close to her most sick children more than anyone else.»

* Mirjana not only prays for unbelievers but she suffers very much for them. Actually she knows what we do not know and often entrusts her concern: «It

is terrible to spend an entire life as if God did not exist. When the moment of death comes and all of one's life has been lived without God, it is terrible. I beg you, pray for them each day because they do not know what awaits them.»

* With respect to the priests, Mirjana adds: «It is easy to establish the difference between a priest who loves the Blessed Virgin and a priest who is not Marian. A Marian priest is able to be recognized by his simplicity, his sweetness, his patience. The intimacy with the Blessed Virgin makes the ♡ more simple.»

Let us continue giving our «YES» to the Blessed Virgin each day so as to be more and more «in her image», as she invites us to do.

Grace and peace, and courage!

Monthly message of the Blessed Virgin of October 25, 1992

«Dear children,

I invite you to prayer now when Satan is strong and wishes to make as many souls as possible his own. Pray, dear children, and have more trust in me, because I am here in order to help you, and to guide you on a new path towards a new life. Therefore, dear little children, listen and live what I tell you, because it is important for you when I shall not be with you any longer, that you remember my words and all I have told you. I call you to begin to change your life from the beginning and that you decide for conversion not with words but with your life. Thank you for having responded to my call!»

The anti-bomb cloud

In Ljubuski the Croatian chief of police received us behind his large desk. He showed such gentleness, his glance was so limpid, his smile so radiant that with his military fatigues, I imagined him willingly running toward his enemy to console him of this war rather than to fire above him...

«Valentin» is well-kmown in Medjugorje. Draga (Ivan's cousin) who served me as interpreter, knows him very well and scrupulously gives him all my questions. He answers very calmly in spite of the gravity of the present time and the great restlessness of all his men due to a large offensive around Mostar these days.

- «How many dead yesterday?
- Nine of our men. But we were able to retake six villages.»

He is like their father; I feel it in his heart.

- «Sister, since I am a military man, I can only report to you what happened on the field. It is true that, in all of this region, Medjugorje and its surroundings have enjoyed a protection which cannot be militarily explained. All our soldiers have observed it. We are here to confirm, not to interpret.»

Then he described to me in detail the cases of unexploded bombs, the fact that there has not yet been anyone killed in Medjugorje, etc. Every four sentences, he was interrupted by a phone call or by the arrival of a message coming from the front.

- «And the testimony of the Serbian pilot?» I asked.

- «What Serbian pilot?»

It had to be me who had to tell him the story when I had come to hear it from his mouth!

He listened to me as he took notes.

- «It is a story everybody knows (it appeared in a local newspaper), but I came to find out from you the details still missing, or those I am not sure of.»

- «Excuse me, Sister, but I cannot tell you anything about this story; I do not know anything about it.»

The intonation in his voice showed that it was that, nothing else... I understood; he will not say anything. A conspiracy of silence? Maybe. Everyone would know the story except him, the chief of police? But my request went very far; undoubtedly it deals with a very special file which will remain secret until the end of the war.

I contained my deception then and found myself facing the Blessed Virgin to deal with the development of the operations before her. In fact I promised her to write in these chapters only the exact truth and for this definite matter, I cannot have access to the original texts.

I must respect my little agreement with her and I will not write here except the essential of which I am sure:

Last May, a Serbian pilot had as his mission to bomb Medjugorje. This man was an atheist. When he came above the plain of Medjugorje, he was unable to release his bomb for reasons that cannot be rationally explained. He released it in a desert environment. That saved his life because while still flying very low his plane was hit by Croatian anti-aircraft fire from the area. (If he had kept his bomb, he would have exploded with his plane.) But his ejection seat permitted him to bail out in a parachute while his plane crashed some kilometers farther. He was then captured by the Croatian Army which kept him in prison, documented his statement, and finally exchanged him with the Croatian prisoners who had been detained by the Serbs as that is usually done.

There you have in substance what took place. Of course, many kinds of details circulated in Medjugorje and the surrounding villages concerning the spiritual reaction of the pilot, the description of the strange phenomenon which hid the village, the depth of the hole made by the bomb which was released in a deserted area, the number of Croatian soldiers the Serbs had to give in exchange for this pilot... but patience, let us wait for the exact text of the statement.

The fact is that the Gospa had preserved her Oasis of Peace by means which for her simple, unexpected, effective, sparing all shedding of blood in one camp as well as the other. She extended her mantle of protection, such a cloud to conceal her treasure before the vehicle of death which threatened it,and we bless her with all our heart for it!

This story is our story. Not only because our «dear Gospa» used all our prayers to protect her Oasis of Peace but also because she shows us how she is able to protect all her oases which are each of our hearts, against the bombs of the Destroyer. What amazes me is to see that in a few seconds, by placing her veil over this village condemned to be «erased from the map», she did more than these endless and costly round tables of politicians who sign treaty after treaty and who cannot prevent hatred from striking its mortal blows. A simple word from her and the bomb was carried away to the desert... There you have the effectiveness of prayer; there you have the power of the saints. That is why on April 25, she recalled the one, unique, incontrovertible strategy of peace: «Only prayer and fasting can stop the war.»

That reminds me of an analogous situation during the Second World War.

In 1944 the American Army began withdrawing from Italy. Based in Foggia, the army air force received orders to bomb the region of San Giovanni Rotondo. Every one knows that there is the convent of Father Pio, but the Americans of the time were far from knowing the existence of this monk endowed with exceptional charisms.

The American colonel directing the squadron of bombers had just taken off when in the sky a large monk appeared to them who held his arms in the form of a cross as if to say «Halt!» The colonel was shocked as never before in his life, and completely stunned, he went back with his squadron. On his return to the base, he told the story of the strange apparition of the monk, which was confirmed by his men. They had him describe precisely the face and the aspect of the monk, and that gave someone the idea of taking him to see Father Pio. He recognized him immediately, and Father Pio confirmed the statements of the colonel. Thanks to his gift of bilocation, he had been able to stop a terrible slaughter. It was from that day on that Father Pio became known in America. This helped him enormously to build his hospital for the «relief of suffering».

Yes, one single man who prays deeply with the heart...

It is so easy at times...

A young couple with two little children lived in our immediate circle. Since they had some common friends with us, we were often led to meet them. The man liked us well, but his wife was a bitter enemy to us. We had wanted to speak to her gently and offer her some small signs of friendship; we encountered a wall! Each time that each of us had to deal with her for little things, he had to catch his breath and prepare himself to be cast like an uncouth, vulgar person.

Of course, it was excellent for a Christian community to have such people to endure, because sanctity develops with more difficulty when «everybody is beautiful; everybody is nice!»

The cause of this hatred? Difficult to say, seeing the enormous difference in culture between her and us. And putting the cards on the table was out of question. The first days after our arrival, she had heard by chance a cassette with the melodies of our office of vespers and she had concluded: «They are Serbs!» Otherwise said in good French: «It is horrible!» Unfortunately, the message of the Gospa «Love your Serb-Orthodox brothers!» she had not heard yet.

That raised in her much less heartlessness than an open mind. Let us not forget that, before the coming of the Gospa, the peasants of Medjugorje lived a thousand leagues from the modern world, and that never had a single stranger gone into this lost village of Herzegovina which had just discovered running water. In a few years, it was necessary for them to pass from the Middle Ages to the concluding twentieth century, nothing astonishing then to find among them certain mixtures a little simple. How could she have been able to guess that in France as in other countries, many Catholics adopted with enthusiasm certain riches of Orthodox tradition, such as the icons, the splendid melodies of its liturgy, the great saints of Russia, etc?

Like many mothers, Ljerka had to leave Medjugorje with her children to take refuge in Croatia with other families of our neighborhood. From time to time the husband soldiers went to pay them a visit and to bring them a little food which they could get for themselves: as much to say a misery!

We were receiving supplies through French trucks[1] , that permitted us to make these poor families of refugees happy. They are crowded sometimes in

---

[1] Our friend Gerard Coulais was one of the most faithful to defy the Croatian routes since the beginning of the war.

a single room and deprived of everything. Cecile had the responsibility of preparing the packages. She had an idea directly from the Holy Spirit. Prepare a package well furnished with baby beds, powdered milk, different supplies and little goodies which console the heart as well as the body; that precisely for Ljerka, our dear «friend». The event was repeated several times in the course of our months of exile.

Then at the beginning of June, we saw Ljerka return... changed! She came toward us with a radiant smile, spoke to us from the abundance of her heart, of her joy to return to Medjugorje, of her acknowledgement of the packages. Since then the shadows have dissipated as through enchantment; a sign of generous love had sufficed, when, according to human justice, we would have been able take her hatred into account to deprive her of our help.

That had not escaped her.

The Gospa, once again, had used the war to cure a soul.

News from Medjugorje, November 1, 1992, Feast of All Saints

Dear Children of Medjugorje,

Praised be Jesus, Delight of all the saints in Heaven!

* Difficult situation in the area of Stolac and Mostar, due to the increase of Serbian troops from Dubrovnik (now liberated). The soldiers of Medjugorje must not leave the country and many are mobilized to help in these fronts. Fortunately our zone is well protected and pilgrimages are more than encouraged.

* Marija and Father Slavko leave on the 12 for Spain and Portugal. The ties with Fatima are increasingly stronger.

* The old people here say: «This war is different from all the others, and worse. In 1940, the front was far from the residences. Now the places of massacre are the cities themselves, the villages or entire populations are exterminated in their own homes.»

Who can survive in the encircled cities?

* From the camp at Doboj, they continue evacuating some prisoners slowly but surely. Thus a girl found herself on a list of liberation without knowing how since neither her parents nor her brother were able to leave. Having been a refugee in Zagreb, she testifies: «In Doboj, we were horribly hungry.» Let us help the Lord to completely empty these camps!

From Sarajevo a woman was able to send a message by amateur radio: «We do not even have a single morsel of bread. We have come to eat grass. In the apartments, the people scrape the wood from their floors in order to make soup. The soldiers seize the convoys of supplies.»

* For Bosnia, the High Commissariat for the Refugees (HCR) anticipates this winter «400,000 dead from cold and from hunger, of whom 100 000 are children». 100 000 innocent children? We are not going to allow that to happen. It is still Jesus who agonizes in them. At the time when Satan wants to possess a maximum number of souls, I propose a counteroffensive on the part of each of us. During this winter, we will be able to replace the activities attached by the daily Mass (real or from desire). We will plunge into the Blood of Jesus, living the distress of all these little ones, beseeching the Father with Jesus to overwhelm by His Spirit the captive souls of Satan. Is Europe not moving? It is the Spirit of God which will open the prisons. The success of this operation depends on our outburst of love. The Gospa told Mirjana: «The greatest privilege which has been given to man on this earth is the Mass.» «It is the strongest of prayers.» «With love, one obtains everything, even the most impossible things.»

Thank you with all my ♡ !

The best way to stop wars?...

Since the war in Bosnia-Herzegovina, many pilgrims have told us: "Here you have a war with bombs, but back home it is worse: hatred has entered our families... we are tearing each other apart even in our own homes."

It is true that the most murderous wars always start in one center of the heart when we develop hatred against our neighbor and we allow bitterness to build up inside year after year.

The Queen of Peace knows this well, She tells us: "Start by loving the people in your own homes because Satan wants to destroy your families, he is very active, especially against the young people." True, Satan knows well that by stirring up misunderstanding and hatred in the families, then like childs play, he can start up wars between people, he can use his prime material for the most important destructions. It is in this way that many families have become true stepping stones of Satan and warehouses for his sinister weapons. On the other hand, families that pray are the high places of disarmament of hatred because the Holy Spirit lives there and works freely and spreads the good perfume of Christ which makes demons flee. It is because of this that for more than twelve years, the Gospa has been asking us to pray in the family. Here, in Medjugorje, we never get tired of telling this to the pilgrims who often, with eyes wide open, tell us: "Prayer in the family?... Impossible!" And the arguments are so good that we could let ourselves be easily convinced. But it is the Gospa who is right, and She knows more than anybody else that nothing is impossible to God.

Albert, fifty, comes for the first time to Medjugorje. The shock of his life: he cries for joy when he discovers he has such a Mother, such a Savior. On the last day of his pilgrimage he learns that the Gospa asks for family prayer. He changes his face and becomes sad.

- But if you knew what my wife said to me before my departure! Injuries, mockeries, threats, it was awful! I am alone in the house with her. Family prayer? It is useless to think of it, she rejects everything completely!

- Albert, I told him, do you believe that the Gospa knows your situation?

- Uh... yes, she should know it.

- Has she said in her message: "Pray in the family except Albert whose situation is completely blocked?"

- Uh... No, I don't think so.

- Do you blieve that she is capable, if she asks you something, to make it possible herself, that which today seems impossible?

- Uh, able of converting my wife? There she would really have to go for it! No way, if you knew my wife!

- She has seen others like her! Are you ready to trust Her?

- I'm ready. OK, but how?

- This is the game plan, you will do exactly as she asks, you know, she is very practical: you will pray at home, without giving great speeches to your wife. You will tell the Gospa. As you see, I do as you say, I pray in the family, but all alone! So we'll make a deal, you take care of my wife (good luck!) and I will take care of your intentions, I will pray for what you ask: for peace in all hearts, for priests, for unbelievers, for the youth, I will pray so that your plans may be fulfilled. I'll take care of your things, and you take care of mine.

Albert decided to do this and added:

- I will come back one day on a pilgrimage, because I know I will need it, but we are broke... in two years, maybe!

Four months later, in a group of pilgrims, who do I see, Albert!

- I can't believe it! You're back!

With his finger he points to a woman in the group.

- It's her! She almost forced me. We didn't have enough money, but nothing could stop her: "We will be able to manage with Providence," she said. So we're here!

- Your wife! It's incredible! Tell me...

- Alright. At home, I persevered in prayer, I was sure that the Gospa would act. One day after several weeks, my wife came in: - Albert, uh, I don't want to disturb you... Could I just sit with you for a while? - OK, sit down, you don't bother me... - Uh, what is this "prayer" thing? - You want me to explain? - Yeah, just to know what you're doing.

Day after day, she came back, in the beginning a bit shy. I spoke to her more and more about God. She couldn't believe what she was hearing, she didn't have at all this image of God. Then, we spoke about Medjugorje, and that finally made it. And then, Albert added, - now Sister, I have a new problem, she prays so much that sometimes I can't keep up!

Queen of Peace, thank you! Like God, you give what you request.

News from Medjugorje, November 15, 1992

Dear Children of Medjugorje,

Praised be Jesus!

* Now it is no longer a secret: the visionary Jakov has made his decision concerning his life. He plans to get married at Easter to an Italian girl. He will be twenty-two years old. With his young spouse, he will live in a new house located near Mirjana's house and Ivan's. Let us pray that they will glorify the Lord by living this very beautiful sacrament!

* In the region, the traditional greeting «Praised be Jesus!»

- «Always Jesus and Mary!» has given place to a very special salutation in the war: «You are alive!» - «Yes, thanks to the Lord, to you also!»

* School has not begun yet in Medjugorje. For some weeks, the parish undertook a very beautiful initiative for the children. Each morning at ten o'clock, they gather to listen to speak about God and pray their rosary for peace. Several among them led the rosary in the evening.

* The streets of Medjugorje swarm now with a large number of children unknown until now; little Croatian refugees welcomed by the village with their mothers. Medjugorje shelters more than twelve-hundred refugees; this increases its population by three quarters. May the Gospa quickly dress their wounds and speak to their heart, because only a small number comes to church.

* The Croatian military offensives are fighting to the fullest these days in order to push back the front. Let us pray so that the Lord comforts all the families, more and more numerous, in their sorrow.

* In an interview, Father Slavko analyzed thus the non-intervention of the

countries which could stop ethnic extermination: «If a country is used to the idea that thousands of its own youth die from drugs or its babies from abortion, how would it stand up to prevent a massacre of five-thousand Croatians here or ten-thousand Muslims there? All destruction and wars take their source from the scorn for life. And peace depends on our conversion to life, our love for life. Without this conversion to life, we will destroy ourselves and we will have allowed others to be destroyed...»

«Dear children, the Gospa tells us, thank God for the beauty and the greatness of the gift of life...» «Thank God because He has created you in such a marvelous way.»

* We do not understand to what extent prayer and fasting are powerful in fighting against this culture of death which is ours, against this modern sickness which rejects life. I learn from the «Mother of Mercy» Association that once they have begun the «chains of fasting», there are four less abortions among the mothers who have been helped. (A chain of fasting consists of 10 people who decide to fast for a mother in distress so that she will keep her baby.) That is what the Gospa wants to do for this war and for our wars.

The Mother of Life loves our life so much!

«Dear children, I love each of you as much as I love my Son. Jesus.»

Grace and Peace!

Monthly message of the Blessed Virgin of November 25, 1992

«Dear children:

Today, as never before, I invite you to pray. May your life become prayer in all its fullness. Without love you cannot pray. Therefore, I invite you to first love God, the Creator of your life, and then you shall also discover and love God in all, as He loves you. Dear children, it is a grace that I am with you. Therefore, accept and live my messages for your good. I love you and, therefore, I am with you to teach you and to guide you to a new life of renunciation and conversion. Only in this way shall you discover God and everything which is far from you now. Therefore, little children, pray. Thank you for having responded to my call.»

IX

Winter-Spring, 1992-1993
Perseverance

News from Medjugorje, December 1, 1992

Dear Children of Medjugorje,

Praised be Jesus, our only Savior, in this sorrowful Advent.

* The cease fire which had left a little respite in Herzegovina was frequently violated; a rain of shells on the villages beyond Mostar.

* Several pilgrims lived in Medjugorje an experience of a very particular kind which is lived in general at the time of death. Suddenly their entire life passed in front of their eyes, as in a film. They could see precisely and clearly each moment of their lives where they had said YES to God and those where they had said NO. Their conscience was overwhelmed by such a light that they saw themselves as though in the «realm of the Holy Spirit» with the darkness of sin and the clarity of given love. They experienced a deep repentance again. All received at the same time a great physical and spiritual healing. Thus a drug addict was completely freed from drugs, and a person who was paralyzed got up from his seat. They had only one desire: to put God and His love in first place in their lives.

And the Gospa challenges us: «Begin to change your lives completely.» Yes, let us not wait to see the film, at the hour of our death... Let us fill the final sequences with ♡ !

* Some countries are no longer coming to Medjugorje. Where have the American, Canadian, Italian pilgrims who used to come so numerous, gone! Is it dangerous?

No, on the contrary! When we see the problems in families, the emptiness in hearts, the distress among the youth... When we see the immense graces distributed here and the profound healings, we say: it is indeed more dangerous for our lives not to come to Medjugorje than to come here!

Is it that the negative advice from certain embassies would carry more weight for us than the pressing invitations from the Gospa? That would be a pity, because one day the apparitions will cease... And is it not through violence that we take hold of the kingdom?

* Do you know that the Blessed Virgin has just appeared again in Fatima and in Lourdes? Actually Marija was in Fatima and Vicka in Lourdes at the end of November. The Gospa had surely joined them there and she must have been very happy about it!

* Thank you for bringing an intense fervor to prayer for this country; the refugees are more and more numerous, often parked like animals where they can. Thousands of families are without any resources; with respect to the prisoners in camps... it is a frightful martyrdom for them.

Fortunately we know that the time of the trial can be shortened through the prayer of the saints.

With all my ♡ ,with you in this difficult struggle and this great hope!

News from Medjugorje, December 15, 1992

Dear Children of Medjugorje,

Praised be Jesus in the night of the maternal womb and praised be His birth in our world!

* Ivan has returned to us from America in good shape, after a good number of gatherings in which he was able to give witness for the Gospa. A great joy for us who go, thanks to him, to find again our evening prayers with the Mother of God on the mountain.

* A survivor from Doboj spoke to me. I think that her survival in camp was due to all your fervent prayers. Having been freed in October, she did not have any more news from her family which had stayed in camp. She said that beside the brutality and hunger, the worst was not to know any more about the outside

world,.to think that no one was looking for them any longer to save them, and that they were completely abandoned in the hands of their enemies. The anguish of the horror without end.

* She told me that because of reprisals she cannot do anything except pray.

* The auxiliary bishop of Split died in a car accident; he was 44. Monsignor Petar Solic was a member of the Commission for Medjugorje. Today it is in the light of God that he knows the reality of Medjugorje, what he has done or what he has not done for it. Let us pray for him and so that he may inspire well his colleagues on the Commission...

* The Gospa avails herself of everything to attract her children and as Marija says: «She is crafty!» It is thus that we see all kinds of drivers and escorts of humanitarian convoys come to her. Very often they know the furniture of bars in their own countries better than that of churches. They follow here a very beautiful path of conversion.

* The situation in Bosnia is worsening from day to day. Even if the war were to stop today, years of humanitarian aid would still be necessary to get the country back on its feet. Serbia does not intend to stop. Seeing her reserves and armaments, she can continue for seven years. For a few dollars a month, thousands of Russians and Bulgarians come to increase her army... But what is this human power against prayer with the heart? Some wind! Thank you for persevering, thank all of you for remaining faithful to the first lines in the humble daily life in order to dismantle hate through prayer.

* The Holy Father calls all of us to a day of prayer for peace in Europe and throughout the Balkans, on January the 1st.

* Some villagers have begun to fast on bread and water in preparation for Christmas. In 1985, the Gospa said: «I ask you to prepare yourselves for Christmas through penance, prayer, and works of charity. Do not attach so much importance to material things for then you will not be able to live Christmas...».

«For Christmas, I ask you to celebrate Jesus together with me. On that day I will give him to you in a very special way...»

How beautiful you are, O Mother of God dressed in gold! We take your Son to hold Him tight in our arms and against our ♡ !

Monthly message of the Blessed Virgin of December 25, 1992

«Dear Children:

Today, I wish to place you all under my mantle, to protect you from every satanic attack. Today is the day of Peace, but throughout the whole world there is much lack of peace. Therefore, I call you to build up a new world of Peace together with me, by means of prayer. Without you, I cannot do that, and therefore I call all of you, with my motherly love, and God will do the rest. Therefore, open yourselves to God's plans and purposes for you to be able to cooperate with Him for peace and for good. And, do not forget that your life does not belong to you, but is a gift with which you must bring joy to others and lead them to Eternal Life. May the tenderness of my little Jesus always accompany you. Thank you for having responded to my call».

News from Medjugorje, January 1, 1993

Feast of the Mother of God
Dear Children of Medjugorje,

Praised be the Child Jesus who accompanies us in His tenderness; praised be Mary His Mother who lays Him in the manger of our ♡ !

* No news regarding military offensives in Herzegovina in these feast days. But in order to stress the very festive Midnight Mass, the soldiers decided to fire all kinds of rounds and explosives in order to replace the traditional explosives.

* All the visionaries are in Medjugorje and Jakov was happy to introduce his young fiancee Anna Lisa who arrived from Italy.

* The Gospa said in a message: «It is on Christmas night that I free the most souls from Purgatory.» All experienced this joy.

And on the evening of Christmas, Marija, Ivan, Vicka and Jakov saw her more resplendent than ever in her dress of gold. Marija told us: «Jesus was also all dressed in gold, because he was enveloped in the dress of His Mother. They were not able to surpass one another!»

Many pilgrims expressed that here they were almost touching heaven.

* As in Bethlehem, the Blessed Virgin is looking for havens of love for her

babies born from the war. Hundreds of young women are the toys of soldiers in concentration camps. Pregnant following rapes, they are released after six months of pregnancy because this way they are not able to abort and they will bring forth little Serbians. Traumatized by this cruelty, many of them reject their «baby-Tchetniks». The Pope has encouraged Christians to help these mothers and to receive these children in Zagreb.

* In Sarajevo, mothers say to themselves with distress: «How long will I be able to nurse my baby? After my last drop, he will die of hunger in my arms, like hundreds already around me...»

* A friend tells us over a ham radio: «We do not even have water to clean the wounds of the wounded.»

* At the time when the little, the poor and the sick pay more than the others the invoice of hatred, why not put into practice and cry out to the world the only two means to stop the infernal machine, are prayer and fast?

* Medjugorje will raise our world. On Christmas night, in spite of the war, joy was here in its fullest. Many young people, more or less unbelievers, experienced the moving catch of the discovery of God-Creator-Love.

At the heart of these bloodied Balkans, Medjugorje is a torch of joy. The Gospa gladdens the ♡ so that they can receive the Savior, so that the tenderness of our little Baby Jesus is used there to its maximum and that we become able to love all mankind. In Medjugorje, the joy of heaven breathes in the sadness of the earth which then disappears. But the Gospa is in search of collaborators everywhere in the world.

A year ago, when Father Slavko instructed a retreat of young people and Marija joined the evening rosary, the Gospa uttered this cry during the apparition: «Dearly beloved, oh, how it would be easy for me to stop the war if I found more people who would pray as you pray!»

In 1992, she did not find enough to stop the war. But, in 1993..., we are not going to leave her without our help!

Dear Gospa, with you we will make out of this year, the year of your victory through love. With you we will fight to death in order to choose love in all circumstances. With the rosary and your joy in us, we will conquer Satan.

Through you, a Savior is born to us!

Revelation to Jelena, January 2, 1993

During a short stay in Medjugorje for Christmas vacation, Jelena opened her heart to us concerning what she has lived these times. She always receives her internal locutions accompanied by internal images, and seems to plunge into a deeper and deeper meditation (all while being a student). She was amazed by the recent discovery revealed to her heart in prayer:

- «I saw that during her life on earth, the Blessed Virgin did not cease to pray the rosary.»

General consternation... I asked:

«How is that possible since most of this prayer was destined to her? She could not even say: I greet myself, Mary, I who am full of grace...!

- Of course not, that is not the case. But she constantly went over the life of Jesus in her heart and her internal look never left him. Now the rosary, for us also, is not anything else but that: with the help of the 15 mysteries, we go over Jesus' entire life (and that of Mary in union with Him) with love in our hearts. That is the true spirit of the rosary, and it is thus that the Gospa calls us to live it.»

News from Medjugorje, January 15, 1993

Dear Children of Medjugorje,

Praised be Jesus!

* As always in January, the priests visit the homes in the village to bless them. Still a truly living tradition here, the Blessed Virgin herself recommended not only to bless our homes but also to put in them blessed articles, in order to keep Satan away from them. In Medjugorje, Christianity again the deep and biblical meaning of the blessing finds. We need it more than ever in these times of combat.

* January is also the least frequented month for pilgrimages, and the visionaries take advantage of it to travel.

Jakov left for Italy; Ivan is leaving on the 17th with Father Slavko for a long apostolic tour in Australia. Marija left with Father Orec for gatherings in Italy. Vicka is in Zagreb; Jelena has rejoined Steubenville (USA) and Mirjana leaves for Switzerland. Thank you for having prayed for the visionaries because the

Gospa relies on them to rekindle our world in a spiritual coma. Isn't it the first case in history where she accompanies the visionaries in her apparitions wherever they go? It is a very special mercy for our time.

* Soldiers from Medjugorje continue to go to the front, but the situation is very peaceful in the whole region. On the contrary, very hard fighting continues in Sarajevo and in central Bosnia in spite of meetings in Geneva which would be able to bring some hope. But for the Croatians, the only sign of peace will be to see a real disarmament on land and not new signatures affixed to documents. They want action, not promises.

Many concentration camps have not yet given up their prisoners, and the «ethnic cleansing» continues its exactions from the heart of a Europe which resembles Pilate washing his hands. The representatives from the High Commissariat for Refugees (HCR) are witnesses of the proceedings of terrorism in order to empty the villages of their inhabitants, pillage, then they burn the houses, but they must see to it that everything is wasted in order to be able to bring some cans of preserves to «displaced persons» (they have orders not to intervene).

* The women who have been raped in the camps and have taken refuge in Croatia are in terrible grief. Many commit abortion because they are ashamed and do not want to have to witness. It is urgent to organize a reception for these women and propositions for adoptions for their little ones. Before this tragedy, there is total judicial emptiness. It is the appropriate time for the «violent of the Kingdom» to take up bold initiatives, to shake laws which allow aborting the child instead of protecting his life. As the Gospa said: «Through love, turn into good everything that Satan wants to destroy and to take for himself.»

* It is in prayer that we have put our hope of change and Medjugorje faithfully continues its ministry in this sense. We know through Ivan that these days, the Gospa calls us to pray more intensely for her intentions (which she keeps secret) because she needs our prayers.

* The commission of inquiry is always out of work because of the war, but that does not stop those who have given their YES to the Queen of Peace, who pursues her plan. Jakov was telling us the other day:

«The sign, I saw it with my own eyes. The Gospa showed it to me. I know the exact date of its coming.»

The unshakable peace of the visionaries shows us that the Gospa knows where she is going and that she holds the world in her hands and in her heart, in the hands of a Queen and in the heart of a Mother!

Happy are we who have her!

Monthly message of the Blessed Virgin of January 25, 1993

«Dear Children!

Today I call you to accept and live my messages with seriousness. These days are the days when you need to decide for God, for peace and for the good. May every hatred and jealousy disappear from your life and your thoughts, and may there only dwell love for God and for your neighbor. Thus, only thus shall you be able to discern the signs of this time. I am with you, and I guide you into a new time, a time God gives you as a grace, so that you may get to know Him more. Thank you for having responded to my call»!

News from Medjugorje, February 17, 1993

Dear Children of Medjugorje,

Praised be Jesus!

* After the wave of departures, returns to Medjugorje are well begun. Vicka, Jakov and Mirjana are with us while Marija and Ivan are expected before the end of the month. It seems that Ivan's tour with Father Slavko in Australia and New Zealand has produced many good fruits. Numerous crowds gathered wherever they went, showing the immense thirst of hearts for a hope which does not deceive.

* The village is still calm. Its reputation of total protection has now reunited the international political milieux, so that the UNO has chosen it to base some 200 Spanish Blue Helmets there, and all their new tanks. They have the mission to protect the humanitarian convoys to Bosnia; this is not logical seeing the distance, but the reason is clear: «It is the most peaceful zone in the country and that is necessary for our men», they say.

With respect to the men in question, they discover with amazement that the Blessed Virgin has been appearing here for eleven years...!! Would The Gospa organize some «wild pilgrimages» for the UNO ?? It is unbelievable to see that atheistic politicians recognize Medjugorje as a sure refuge, at the time when so many Christians in the country do not yet see in it «The Oasis of Peace» given by Heaven. Dear Gospa, a point for you!

* Vicka told us yesterday: «We are living a time of grace, but many people do not understand it. They have placed fear of the war in the first place; they

allow themselves to be caught by material concerns, money... they are blinded and they do not even see the proof that there are no deaths or destruction here. No, it is necessary to put the messages in the first place; only then will we be able to discover how this time is a time of grace!»

* A member of Ivan's prayer group explains: «What counts in prayer, are not the extraordinary things. It is the daily faithfulness and perseverance for, just as the plant needs its drop of water each day in order to live and grow, likewise, we need our drop of water to live, and this drop we receive in daily prayer. Without this drop, we will die little by little. There you have what the Gospa teaches us».

Dear Gospa, how can we not say to you YES with all our ♡ !

Monthly message of the Blessed Virgin of February 25, 1993

«Dear Children:

Today I bless you with my motherly blessing and invite you all to conversion. I wish that each of you decides for a change of life and that each of you works more for the Church, not through words and thoughts but through example, so that your life may be a joyful testimony for Jesus.

You cannot say that you are converted because your life must become a daily conversion. In order to understand what you have to do, little children, pray and God will give you what you concretely have to do, and where you have to change. I am with you and place you all under my mantle. Thank you for having responded to my call.»

News from Medjugorje, March 1, 1993

Dear Children of Medjugorje,

Praised be Jesus, Who draws us to His victory.

* How does one describe the political imbroglio of Bosnia-Herzegovina, where the situation becomes more difficult each day? From a human point of view it is not possible to envisage that Serbs, Muslims, and Croats can first of

all live together; the majority of the towns are mixed! In order to expel the Muslims from their homes, the Serbs now use the protected corridors of humanitarian aid, like at Siporo where 2000 people underwent «ethnic cleansing». It continues inexorably... In the midst of this drama, zone number 8 (proposed in the carving out) is exempted from conflicts. It is the only one, and it is the one of Medjugorje...

Father Slavko has returned very happy from his tour with Ivan in Australia. Beyond the discovery of kangaroos and monkeys, they give thanks for the 150,000 people who were touched by the message of Medjugorje.

* Because of the confusion which is raging in Croatia and the overwhelming problem of the refugees, it is not yet possible to adopt the «children-victims» abroad. For the time being, only a deep prayer can make things progress. The forces of evil target, of course, the most vulnerable and the combat has to be won, first of all, in the invisible. The women who have been raped represent gold for the newspapers and magazines, without speaking of the most sordid businesses tied to abortion. The solutions of aid are going to germinate in place; our fast and our prayers are able to do such.

* Vicka returned from a big conference in Holland, suffering from the flu and feverish, but radiant. With Father Petar and an Italian who works for the drug addicts, she gave witness of the tenderness of the Blessed Virgin and her concern for young people. Among the visionaries, Vicka is undoubtedly the nearest to those who suffer and the most active one to visit them, console them. In Medjugorje, she frequently visits certain young people who have quit drugs in order to take up their lives again under the mantle of the Gospa and she represents a living hope for them.

* It is beautiful to see that for the visionaries nothing is really a misfortune, if it is not to be away or separated from God. Watching them makes us almost forget the war. «With the Gospa, they say, we experience such security!» They entrust themselves blindly to her, and their peace is an open window in heaven.

Mirjana, like Vicka or Jakov, tells us: «When the Gospa asks us for something, we do not ask her why she asks us for it. We do it only because she asks us for it. She, she knows why, and that is sufficient».

What a cure for our rationalism!

Adherence of the heart is more effective than our thoughts and it is the beginning of true joy. The leitmotif of the Blessed Virgin during these months of war is the invitation to this joy of the ♡.

Admirable Mother, Queen of Peace, pray for us!

News from Medjugorje, March 15, 1993

Dear Children of Medjugorje,

Praised be Jesus!

* The hills of Podbrdo and Krizevac produce their first crocus, but if nature obeys its Creator well, men don't. Daily shells over Mostar, with their retinue of destruction. Near Stolac, the Serbs have reinforced their position and the Croats are expecting a severe offensive. This threatens a key bridge for the supply convoys to Sarajevo.

* Medjugorje extremely calm. Father Laurentin is with us. Many pilgrims will be here for Easter; no problems in getting here (plane, boat, Adriatic coast). Come without fear to draw at this fountain of graces!

* Some pilgrims have asked how to conquer distractions in prayer. Mirjana answered them: «When distractions come to me during the rosary, I stop and I speak to the Gospa about my distractions. That frees me. Then I take up my rosary in peace...»

* Vicka has left us for Chicago and Los Angeles. It is her first long trip since the war... She will return around the 20th, by way of Germany.

* Father Slavko has taken advantage of the long Australian travels to write a new book. The theme of it is the adoration of the Blessed Sacrament which the Blessed Virgin has so much recommended in her messages. How to live it with the heart?

* It is a whole continent that has welcomed Ivan and Father Slavko. Actually, the cardinal of Australia had requested all the bishops to give them a good welcome everywhere! ... Well done, Australia!

* For the visionaries, it is a great joy to convey the words of the Blessed Virgin, but it is at the same time a real suffering. Especially for Marija who gives the message for the world each month. Father Slavko related to us that one day she dissolved into tears after having delivered to him her poor little piece of paper after the apparition. (8/21/86)

- «Why these tears, Marija...??

- These words are nothing. I betrayed the message. I am going to ask the Gospa to choose another visionary to transmit her messages to the world...

- But why? You have written very well, without errors!

- When the Blessed Virgin said: «Know, dear children, that I love you immensely (without measure))», such an intensity came from her look! I truly experienced in my heart her infinite love for each one of us. It is impossible to put this experience into words. The people are not going to understand all her tenderness. These words are nothing compared to what she gives!»

Dear Gospa, we want to touch you beyond words!

«I was four years old and I saw her!» March 18, 1993

In December 1982, the Gospa had promised Mirjana to appear to her once a year, her birthday (March 18) and no longer daily because she had received her ten secrets.

On this March 18, 1993, I suddenly remember this detail and we have just the time to get ready to be with Mirjana on time. All kinds of photographers and journalists had already squatted the best places but Divine Providence moved me to two meters from Mirjana, a little in front, although I could attentively observe her face. We were all packed together like sardines, in this very small place, without beauty, and ...without ventilation. Then the heavens opened and Mirjana raised her eyes toward the Mother of God and the Queen of the whole world.

For seven minutes, we attended to the moving dialogue between these two women, these two mothers... The warmth of the Blessed Virgin was so strong, so intense, so palpable that my heart was raised and I cried with amazement while Mirjana let two large tears flow out of joy, she would tell me later. Both of them prayed for unbelievers, and I perceived in my heart thousands of tombs open up to the prayer of the Mother of God. I perceived beings covered with darkness, allowing themselves to join again through her and to be covered with light. The invisible realities cried out stronger than the visible ones, and I read on the beautiful face of Mirjana the splendid work of salvation about to be accomplished. Earth is the waiting room of heaven, but today, the walls are of glass and the windows allow the penetration of perfumes that it is not possible for human words to describe[1].

---

[1] Before we left Mirjana's house, Marco, her husband, gave us each a copy of the message given by the Blessed Virgin during the apparition. This message was then typed and presented by Father Slavko, Marco's uncle. Here it is: "Dear children, my wish is this: give me your hands; thus I will be able to carry you like a mother on the right path. In this way I will be able to carry you to your father. Open your hearts and let me enter. Pray for I am with you in prayer. Pray, so that I will be able to guide you. I will lead you to peace and to happiness."

The true first lines of the front are here. The most real combats of the war, the true victories, it is here that they are played. And the true trophies, they are invisibly carried by little peasants without culture or diploma but who in the simplicity of their heart pray the Our Father with the Mother of God and with all those who in the world unite their voices to theirs.

I will never forget this apparition. However, after three and a half years, I have often seen Marija and Ivan in ecstasy. But today I said to myself: If I had been an atheist, in no time I would have been driven into the faith in God more surely than a hurricane over Florida!

In 1981 the Gospa had said: «May those who do not see believe as if they saw.» And Father Jozo likes to add: «Each one of us is a visionary. A visionary of the heart!»

At times the Gospa likes to show herself secretly to innocent, little beings (hush! Do not repeat it to anyone!) She likes that. That reminds me of a little girl I know, Chirstelle, from Le Mans city, in France. She was four years old then. She had come to Medjugorje with her family for the 5th of August 1988, the birthday of the Blessed Virgin. On the night of the 4th to the 5th of August, she went to Apparition Hill, to participate with her parents in Ivan's prayer group. The songs with the guitar rocked her; she fell asleep on the rocks... At the time of the apparition, she woke up gently and said before Cyrill Auboyneau who was in prayer:

- «I am afraid of the Blessed Virgin!»

Then she began to weep while taking refuge on her sister's lap. She disturbed everyone with her tears, just at the time when the most perfect silence reigned over the crowd concentrated on the presence of the Gospa. After the apparition, Ivan related in Croatian the coming of the Blessed Virgin and what she said. Then everyone descended. Cyrill, who had heard the words of the girl, joined the family and Pierre Godbert for refreshments in the house of the pilgrims. The father was complaining: You have not been nice, Christelle! Why did you cry so loudly? You disturbed everyone!

- She wanted to take me away; I was afraid!

- Afraid of whom?

- Of the Blessed Virgin. She wanted to take me!»

Silence. Everyone swallowed their saliva and Cyrill innocently asked:

- «Did you see the Blessed Virgin?

- Of course! (She thought that everyone could see her.)

Silence again...

- How was she?

- She was beautiful!

- And what else?

- She had a beautiful yellow dress (on feast days the Gospa appears with a golden dress but Christelle did not know the word «golden».)

- Yellow like?»

Christelle was searching, saw a bottle of champagne on the table and cried out:

- Like the cork! (wrapped in golden paper)

- And what else, tell us, continued Cyrill.

- She had a cloth on her head (Christelle did not know the word «veil»); an all white cloth...

- And her hair?

- Her hair, black.

- And her eyes?

She hesitated and looked for a point of reference.

- Her eyes... like those of Mr. Golbert! (Suddenly P. Godbert put his nose on his plate and large tears began to flow while he repeated: «She could not have given me a more beautiful gift!») It is necessary to state clearly that Pierre has very beautiful blue eyes...

And Christelle added:

- She had her feet hidden!

It was her child's way of saying that one did not see the feet of the Blessed Virgin because they were hidden by the white cloud on which she was.

- She had her hands separated, far, far...»

- And Christelle stretched her two little arms as much as possible as if to touch the two walls at the same time. Everything confirmed, without her knowing it, the description of the visionaries.

Now Christelle is eight and the other day her mother told me: «She is just like the other children; she is becoming a little mischievous. But she loves praying very much and having others pray, even in school. As far as our garden is concerned, it is impossible to keep flowers. Everything is gathered by Christelle.

- «It is for the Blessed Virgin», she tells us. We leave her; we see that she has a special intimateness with the Blessed Virgin.

In Medjugorje, many other children have seen the Blessed Virgin. One day, a little boy of three was weeping bitterly at the bottom of the hill. Inconsolable!

- But, my dear, what is wrong with you?

- I want to return there!

- Where?

- Up there!

- But why?

- I want to see her again; I want to see her again!

May every Christian, layman or consecrated, come and see with his ♡ what these children have seen with their eyes!

Monthly message of the Blessed Virgin of March 25, 1993

«Dear Children:

Today like never I call you to pray for peace; peace in your hearts, peace in your families and peace in the whole world, because Satan wants war, wants lack of peace, wants to destroy all which is good. Therefore, dear children, pray, pray, pray. Thank you for having responded to my call!»

Fax from Medjugorje, April 1, 1993

Dear Mama, Dear Tonton, Dear Kiki,
Praised be Jesus who breaks the bolts of death!

* In this waiting for Easter, all the visionaries think again of Good Friday 1988 when the Gospa came with Jesus crowned with thorns, stained with blood, his robe torn... She said then: "I have come with my Son so that you see how much he has suffered for you." He Himself was silent but Vicka confided to me that His look was more than a word of love...

* According to Ivan, on the mountain as she did in Australia, the Gospa invites us to pray for sinners. In response we could all pray the large novena before Mercy Sunday (April 18) when Sister Faustina will be beatified so that the great sin of war will end and every sin against life as Father Slavko said.

* Father Slavko announced the youth Festival the first five days in August as each year.

* The visionaries are more and more humorous. A pilgrim asked Mirjana if on the days of fast one could even take some coffee with sugar in the morning...? Yes, answered Mirjana, quickly before the Gospa wakes up!"

* The angels we sent into the concentration camps worked well. Overwhelming testimonies have reached us like this priest from Bosnia, who was cruelly tortured, who said: "It was extraordinarily beautiful when we, joined to pray for our executioners...". Because of reprisals, these marvelous fioreti are still held secret. Let us continue helping the prisoners through our

inventions of love. There are still thousands of them. Doboj continues!

* Ivan, Mirjana and Ivanka foresee a conference in the United States in May. For Ivan it will be a long two months apostolic tour that will take him as far as Japan.

* I had never seen Mirjana so beautiful as last March 18 at the time of her annual apparition. Her face melted with tenderness before the Gospa. Even if we could not capture this secret dialogue between heaven and earth, the warmth of joy was so strong that everybody cried. Mirjana entrusted to us: I was indescribably happy." The Blessed Virgin did not speak of any secret that time. She prayed for unbelievers.

In the message given to Mirjana, an image struck me. If the Blessed Virgin wishes us to give her our hands, our two hands, it is because one hand is not sufficient for her to lead us to Jesus. Who do we take both hands from? From a baby who does not yet stand on his own two feet, or from a being who is very handicapped and cannot walk. The Gospa knows our miseries; then, in her humility, she walks before us backwards in order to allow the dialogue...

Dear Gospa, how right Jesus was in choosing you!

News from Medjugorje, April 15, 1993

Dear Children of Medjugorje,

Praised be Jesus; He is risen!

* Exactly a year ago, our Easter resembled a great Good Friday here... But what joy this year to see the crowds returning to Medjugorje, and after the evening apparition with Ivan, rivers of lights descended from the mountain, (little lamps of pilgrims). All the visionaries were present in Medjugorje.

* Jakov married Anna-Lisa in the church on Easter Sunday. Father Slavko blessed the marriage. Everyone was touched by the pure and childlike joy of the young married couple. No honeymoon; it is not the tradition here but the wife comes to live in her husband's house of whom she discovers for the first time. She is going to learn Croatian; I hope that she will be more gifted than I am!

* Our bishop Paul Zanic is in hospital in Split, in "intensive care" because of a serious heart problem. Through our intensive and loving prayers, may the Gospa visit and comfort him!

* The nearest fronts are very calm, even in Stolac.

* Mirjana continues teaching us. She says that each prayer made by

unbelievers is, for the Gospa, like a tear one dries on her face.

Mirjana says that when she was working at the Atlas Agency, she had a colleague, an ex-policeman, who uttered a blasphemy every third word. She made no remarks and actually ignored him. But she prayed very much for him in secret. The first month, nothing had changed, but the second month, after each blasphemy he added "Oh, excuse me, Mirjana!". On the third month, the blasphemies had disappeared and now this man is a member of her prayer group on Thursday...

In 1984 the Gospa had told her: "With prayer, you can obtain everything".

* While talking with to visionaries, we have learned that the Blessed Virgin had often pushed them to do spiritual reading and especially the lives of the saints. It is true that the greatest victories are won by the saints. As Satan told the Curé of Ars: If I found only three like you in France, I would not be able to put my feet there any more." (Straight to the point, who want to be the other two...) I have seen some saints even recently in the poorest homes of Medjugorje; those no one visits and who, nevertheless, shelter some treasures of prayer and real mystical life. A needy widow confided to me with her humble look: "I see the Gospa every day in my heart. I know that everything that I tell her, she hears and she grants it." And she was radiant with joy.

Mother of the risen One, give us the beauty of the saints!

Monthly message of the Blessed Virgin of April 25, 1993

Dear Children:

Today I invite you all to awaken your hearts to love. Go into nature and look how nature is awakening and it will be a help for you to open your hearts to the love of God the Creator. I desire to awaken love in your families so that where there is unrest and hatred, love will reign and when there is love in your hearts, then there is also prayer. And, dear children, do not forget that I am with you and I am helping you with my prayer that God may give you the strength to love. I bless you and love you with my Motherly love. Thank you for having responded to my call.

News from Medjugorje, May 1, 1993

Dear Children of Medjugorje,

Praised be Our God the Creator!

* The buds have blossomed and the vines free their little leaves. Nature is splendid and consoles us with many things.

* According to Vicka the Blessed Virgin shows herself to be more concerned with the situation in the world than with that of Bosnia Herzegovina, our prayer for peace has pleased her more than we think.

* Like last year, a "Walk for Peace" is anticipated on June 24 from Humac to Medjugorje (15 kilometers). Departure time 11:00 o'clock, Archbishop Franic will accompany the walk and will celebrate the Mass in the evening. It would be beautiful for each group to bear the banner of its country in order to honor the Gospa. (Other initiatives for peace can be undertaken elsewhere by those who will not be able to come).

* Very painful last fifteen days in the country. It is very difficult to have the truth on the secret agreements between the Serbs and such and such Muslim faction against the Croats and inversely for the key territories. The blood is now running between Muslims and Croats. The center of Mostar is again closed because snipers are killing those who pass by. In Konica (Bosnia), some Muslims took three Franciscans and religious as hostages, making use of them as living shields. The latter could be freed but the atmosphere is filled with anxiety.

* Monsignor Zanic is better; he underwent a heart operation. He is going to stay in Split.

* Marija left us for an apostolic program of eight days in Italy.

* I asked Mirjana:

- "For whom especially does the Gospa give messages here in Medjugorje?"

She vehemently answered me:

- "The Gospa wants to touch the hearts of all her children through her messages. She is mother of all, and it is the whole world that she desires to reunite."

Then here is my proposition: Operation "Fire through Divine"

All of us have in our cupboards some cassettes (or some books) containing the messages which are threatened with sterility if no one has used them for six months. Let us prepare a packet for the Gospa. She will transform these small dusty pieces of plastic into small very powerful generators of light, of high intensity for the darkest nights. Let us stand then in front of a school, university, a supermarket, and distribute our little generators to young people. These young people to whom no one, no one speaks of God.

Thank you for the saints of the year 2000 whom you are going to bear... They will be your lawyers before the throne of God!

The young people of the country are in great distress. To expatriate oneself is a wound which will always bleed for a Croatian heart and to stay means "a blocked future, a threatened survival", especially in the cities. Drugs circulate more and more, even Medjugorje is touched. They are sick and tired of going to the front because of this absurd war. I beg you to pray for them.

The other day, at the front in Stolac, some soldiers from Medjugorje were talking by radio with Serbs who were posted exactly three hundred meters further away. (They got along well after months of being face to face!). The Serbs would say: "Come to us and kill our leaders. We will also go with you to kill your leaders and then finally we will be able to live in peace together as before!"

This short cut is significant...

But it is not exact. Peace will come when we will say truthfully: "Jesus, come to me and be my only Leader. Be my Shepherd". Then the wolves will not enter into the country to rape, to slaughter, and destroy any longer.

If I were a little Therese of Lisieux or a Sister Faustina, devoured with love, then Satan would sink down to the bottom. But... It is not too late!

Grace and peace!

PS: Next news - May 15, 1993.

Author's Note

Perhaps some readers will be tormented by doubt in the presence of certain accounts, the multiplication of food, for example, or every other occasion when the Divine Providence obviously manifested itself. Let these readers be reassured: I have made a serious effort to say only the truth. I also add that these acts are only a small part of the goodness of God which I have been able to experience or verify in the course of these last fifteen years in the bosom of our community. It is the normal Christian life. Is it not normal for the living God to make miracles for the people who trust in Him? Just prior to the war, the Gospa had said to us: "Pray, live my messages, and then you will see the miracles of God in your daily life" (March 25, 1992). Nevertheless, in case of persistent doubt, it is always possible to come to Medjugorje to carry a serious inquiry with first hand witnesses. The eleven refugees[1] who were able to eat the meat of the cow at noon and evening will be happy to tell you what taste this "multiplied" meat had...

---

[1] Distributed in their village of Pocitelj, thirty minutes from Medjugorje.

In Conclusion...

We will leave these pages incomplete because not only is the war not ended but in the course of these last months I have understood that in these painful events, we have been living a true beginning. A beginning of an evil which is going to still spread or the beginnings of a larger spiritual upheaval of our times, of these times which perhaps are the last? The answer depends on you, dear friend of Medjugorje, as it depends on me. The Evil One said one day to the Cure of Ars: "If in France there had only been three like you, I would not have been able to put my feet there!" Accept then, with me, to be the other two saints still lacking and not only in France? If you decide for the "YES", then I calmly conclude this book with a prophecy: "Dear reader, the Gospa's peace plans will not find any more obstacles for their realization; the war is going to end soon."

We are sure that there is no problem with the victory of peace over hatred and its diabolical inventions. We know from the Blessed Virgin herself that with Medjugorje she is going to accomplish everything that she has wanted to realize through the secrets begun at Fatima (Message of August 25, 1991). It is a matter of the triumph of her Immaculate Heart. But how many physically and morally bloody years will the world of today have to go through before the victory of Mary, the one who will crush the head of the Serpent? Admirable Mother: she does not reveal to us "the time and the moment"; she does not play the "Madam Son" or other glaucous prophetess, but she raises our hearts and our spirits in order to solidly establish them in the joy of conquering love. "A joy I cannot describe with words, says Vicka, but which I can only live with my heart."

I caught this remark filled with humor uttered by Daniel-Ange after a few days spent in Medjugorje with us, on listening to the heart of his Mother: "With her it is always joy, joy and still joy! We ask ourselves whether she is really up to date on the situation; if she ever watches television!"

Precisely! Her joy comes from her knowledge of the WHOLE situation, in its present and future trajectory, and she already contemplates in heaven the weight of glory attached to each drop of blood shed on earth, to each secret distress of a heart, lovingly offered by the Church. During her life she contemplated the water changed into wine, then wine changed into blood, then the blood changed into glory just as it flowed from the wounds of her Son, and that still flows in the least of her own.

Sin, with its consequences of death, will pass, while love will always last. Certainly, the mystery of iniquity obtains an unequaled paroxysm from our days. Indeed it is necessary for us to take note of the expressions of the Gospa: "Today as never before..." because she sees the invisible and she wants to warn us. And it is indeed evident that Satan is still going to blacken the picture even more before he gives way. Mirjana knows it. I asked her one day:

- "Do you not experience a great solitude, since you must carry the weight of the ten secrets without being able to talk to anyone about them?

- Yes, I often feel very lonely, with my secrets. But, fortunately, the Gospa helps me. For with everything that I know, if she did not help me, I would not be able to remain normal."

Curiously she is the visionary who confuses the pilgrims the most by the extraordinary peace that flows from her!

New Mauthausen, Dachau or Auschwitz have been quietly established in the heart of Europe in astounding impunity. The very same which made Nuremberg remain paralyzed before the new criminals of war.

We were waiting for the Europe of Robert Schuman, the Europe of the Rights of Man and the Rights of God, but it seems that we have undergone another reality. A certain culture of death has spread and France has been touched by it!

Those words of Marthe Robin come to mind: "...But then she (France) will cry to God, and the Blessed Virgin will come to save her. She will take up again her role as older daughter of the Church; she will live a very strong Pentecost of love and her influence will be extended again all over the world..."

The Blessed Virgin? The Queen of Peace indeed!

Recently, I lived an event rich in meaning. I found myself in a church where, a little before midnight, I was praying with two brothers. Outside it was pitch dark. Suddenly we heard cries and calls for help. We went out to see where they came from. A young man had just fallen inadvertently into the river bed two meters deep. He could have shattered his spinal column.

His first intention was good and legitimate. He wanted to go for a walk, cool. But what do our good and sincere intentions weigh, if we walk in darkness, if our eyes cannot discern the trappings of the night?

The Gospa knows that, and her bosom of a mother turns. Does she not offer Medjugorje to us precisely so that her children do not walk in darkness any longer, even if it is pitch dark in our world? Through her radiant school of love, through the extraordinary power of cure of hearts which she distributes in Medjugorje and from Medjugorje, she is the one who comes very concretely to our aid. Opposing our culture of death, it is she who promises the shipwrecked hope and love, by millions, to rise and to find again the delicious taste for life. And it is only a beginning!

Then why this war?

This war is the most convincing of confirmations for the grace of Medjugorje: there where millions of children of God are born to life, where the mother has given birth to them and continues giving birth to them, how can we be astonished that new Herods arise, repeating the massacre of the innocents?

How to be astonished at the black rage of Satan, the Homicide that as such the Dragon of the Apocalypse, holds himself before the Woman in labor, "ready to devour her child as soon as he is born"? How can we be astonished that this high place of birth of the "Saints of the year 2000" be encircled by a river of blood?

Medjugorje: the Bethlehem of the new millennium.

How can we be astonished also that poor and rich from all nations come there so numerous, loning irresistibly, to learn from Mary how to pray with the heart?

In order to learn from Mary how to pray with the heart?

No, the Herods will not stop love! For the thousands of martyrs who, this winter, will die from the cold, hunger and distress hardly an hour from Medjugorje, there you have, dear friends of Medjugorje, the innocent victims who, with Jesus and the Blessed Virgin pay the price of blood so that all of us without exception become saints; these saints formed by Mary and who will shine like suns.

Is the most profound, visceral, shooting, most vertiginous desire of the heart of man not to have the fullness of love in him?

This fullness; there you have holiness.

Let us not be mistaken with happiness! For the Gospa promises it to us. Our happiness will conquer the war; our holiness will crush death. And the day to begin is today, not tomorrow.

Unfinished May 1, 1993
in Bijakovici

APPENDIX I:

To receive the monthly message given by Our Lady in Medjugorje to Marija for the world, please call:

Alabama	205-666-6279
	205-672-2000
	205-672-9622
Arizona	602-225-1970
	602-234-9850
Arkansas	501-855-3787
	800-235-6279
California	213-896-2999
	408-867-4673
	415-321-6279
	415-755-9396
	503-345-9403

	818-798-3033
	818-773-3060
	714-239-9955
	800-628-3440
Spanish	213-896-1945
Span/Eng	809-872-2112
Colorado	303-329-6785
Connecticut	203-745-3189
Florida	305-662-9542
Span/Eng	305-362-7314
	813-324-4192
	813-522-6322
	904-455-6763
Georgia	800-245-9846
Idaho	208-326-5805
Illinois	708-916-8290
Iowa	515-277-8646
Kansas	913-383-7454
Kentucky	502-339-7777
Louisiana	504-595-6920
	504-949-5104
Maryland	301-275-2920
Massachusetts	413-665-7774
	508-342-9250
	617-639-0080
	508-371-1235
Michigan	517-783-5552
	616-375-6279

	313-544-4730
Missouri	913-383-7454
Nebraska	402-455-6279
Nevada	702-454-6279
New Jersey	201-667-6279
	201-991-3255
Spanish	201-991-3403
New Mexico	505-292-2079
New York	212-547-7729
	516-887-6279
	515-671-5144
	516-484-4030
	516-248-3044
	516-671-5144
	914-682-8907
Spanish	718-277-6727
Ohio	216-941-0870
	419-385-5841
	614-283-6338
	513-575-4844
Oregon	503-345-9304
	503-774-9879
Pennsylvania	215-544-6279
	412-538-5700
	717-586-4323
Rhode Island	401-944-5683
Tennessee	615-327-3322
	615-329-3332

Texas	214-233-6279
	713-465-4564
	512-225-6279
	713-265-2541
Spanish	214-596-6279
Virginia	202-338-4564
	202-529-6279
	804-296-7522
Washington DC	202-529-6279
Wisconsin	414-784-4200
	608-534-6683
Canada	800-344-2836
Canada Toronto	416-252-6279
Lithuanian	416-766-6279
England	034-289-3230

The author would like to express her gratitude to "Mary's People" for the list previously cited. Their address is: Twin Circle Publishing, 12700 Ventura Blvd. Suite 200, Studio City, CA 91604, 1-800-548-6465

Several magazines are publishing the News that Sr. Emmanuel sends from Medjugorje on a regular basis. Please contact the Medjugorje Centers in your country.

APPENDIX II:

MAPS

MAP NR. 1 : THE FORMER YUGOSLAVIA

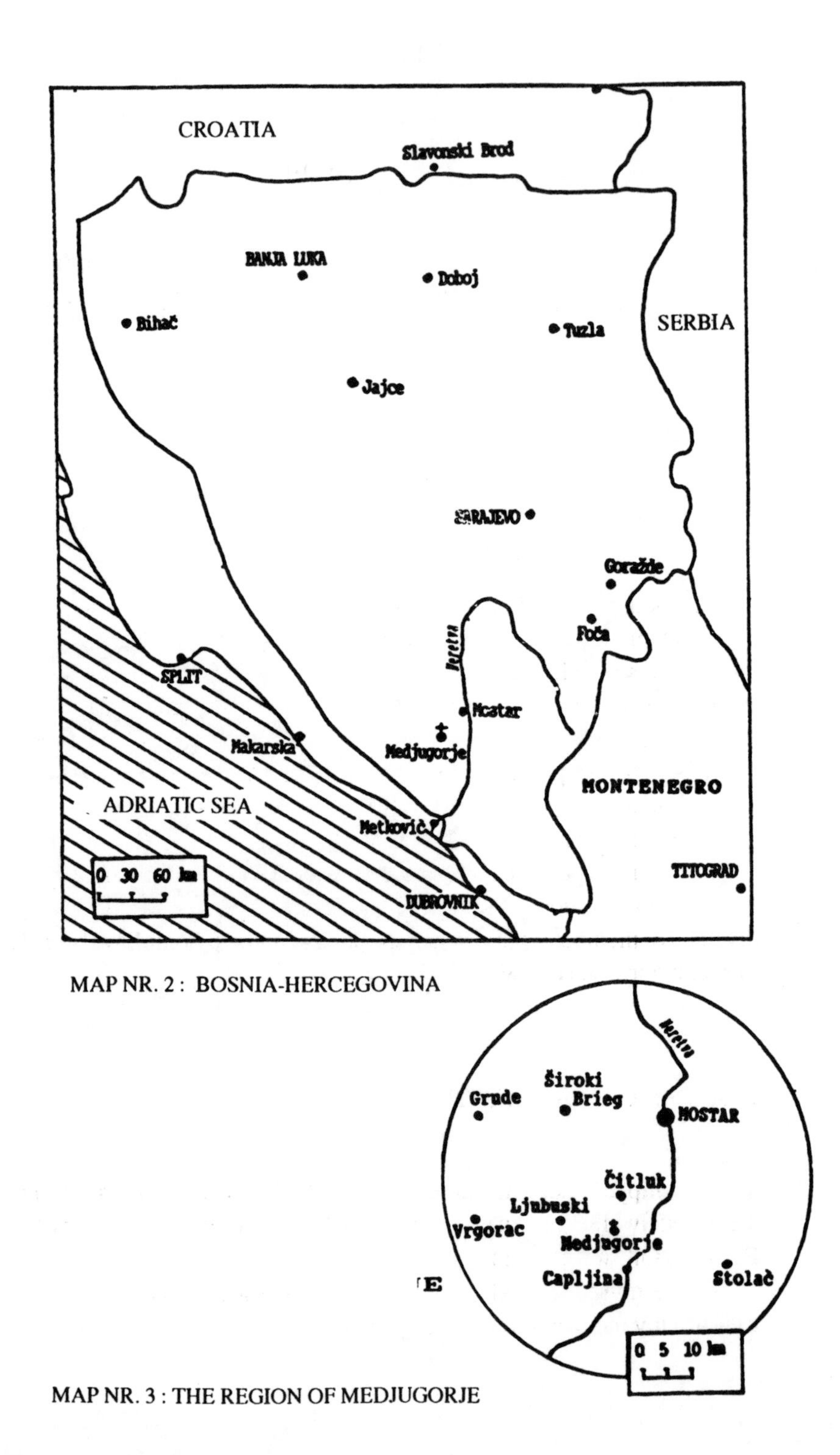

MAP NR. 2 : BOSNIA-HERCEGOVINA

MAP NR. 3 : THE REGION OF MEDJUGORJE

APPENDIX III:

Who are the "Children of Medjugorje"?

A FAMILY

Were you motivated by Medjugorje, were you touched by a pilgrimage, a book, a conference... and you experience the need to develop this grace by joining other people who have also been conquered by the Queen of Peace?

Do you perceive the urgent appeal from our world ravaged by darkness, and you desire to work actively on the side of the Blessed Virgin to live and with her spread the true peace of heart and the numerous treasures of Medjugorje?

Do you wish to hasten the fulfillment of her plans and you are seeking concrete means for it?

Then you are the welcomed one among the "Children of Medjugorje" that receive you with joy. This family is directed by Laymen and by a great diversity of members in the French speaking countries. Some have been living in Medjugorje since 1989.

IT ALL BEGAN AUGUST 23, 1983...

Dr. Philippe Madre (Community of the Beatitudes) and Father Emiliano Tardif received a private message from the Blessed Virgin, delivered by Marija Pavlovic following the apparition:

"I have myself invited each of you to this place because I need you to transmit my messages to the whole word."

This request which comes from heaven is the founding word of the family of the "Children of Medjugorje". The Gospa is counting on us!

3 GOALS

* THE ESTABLISHMENT OF A FRENCH SPEAKING SPIRITUAL CENTER WHEN THE LOCAL SITUATION PERMITS IT.

This center will comprise a cordial place of prayer where one will be able to meditate away from the crowds. It is there also that the will presented a clear explanation of the messages which the Blessed Virgin has given since 1981, so that each one can understand the wishes that our Mother expresses in Medjugorje and answer them wholeheartedly. This will be an opportunity for all to enter her school and understand how much she wants us in order to fulfill her plan for all of humanity.

This center will guarantee all kinds of spiritual services for the pilgrims with external and internal meeting places, little rooms for private receptions, a selling place where to find books, audio and video cassettes, different kinds of information, an audiovisual room...

Thanks to the generosity of the first "Children", we have been able to acquire some very beautiful land for this center, only six minutes from the church and ten minutes from the homes of the visionaries... Thanks to Divine Providence!

We will not provide any lodging! Medjugorje is well provided.

* SOME INITIATIVES IN OUR COUNTRIES

Their goal is to help the Queen of Peace bring together a maximum number of children under her mantle. For that we have already:

- Published all her messages in the book "Words from Heaven"
- Recorded eight audio-cassettes on Medjugorje
- Organized conferences with different witnesses
- Started the monthly messages on minitel and telephone answering machines
- Accomplished a twinning in order to help a village in Croatia
- Circulated attractive leaflets for those who do not know Medjugorje
- Brought about prayer vigils here and there for peace
- Spread the novena asked for by the Blessed Virgin in August 1991

- Guaranteed regular transmission of news from the village with the help of minitel and other answering services
- Supported humanitarian aid and this is only a beginning...

* AN INFORMATION LETTER

A publication was sent free to the "Children of Medjugorje" every two months. You will find news of Medjugorje in it: the principal messages, our plans, announcement of conferences, the life of the visionaries, suggestions of personal approaches toward the Blessed Virgin; thus you will remain united in heart with the open network in place and with all the "Children of Medjugorje."

This letter is free, thanks to the help each one sends according to his generosity.

3 COMMITMENTS

To become a "Child of Medjugorje" is a decision which is taken in prayer because to work in the works of God often requires courage and tenacity. A triple commitment is offered to you:

* PRAY EVERY DAY so that the plans of the Gospa in Medjugorje be fully accomplished and that Satan cannot thwart them in anyway. Be in charge of one of the six visionaries by saying a prayer to the Holy Spirit or a decade of the rosary, so that he will become a saint. A picture of him will be mailed to you on simple request.

* CIRCULATE around you the brochures, leaflets and cassettes which are recommended to you on Medjugorje in order to let the messages be known to all those who are waiting for them to be converted; use creative imagination!

* MATERIALLY SUPPORT the construction of the Center and the other initiatives for the Gospa. Each one gives with joy and according to his generosity in a punctual and regular manner. Thanks in advance to all of you, instruments of Divine Providence!

It goes without saying that each "Child of Medjugorje" is taken in prayer before the Blessed Virgin. Your prayer intentions are given to the visionaries who entrust them to Mary at the time of the apparition. You can send them to us at this address:

Children of Medjugorje[1], Post Restante 88266 Medjugorje, Croatia
(Do not send your subscriptions or your gifts to Medjugorje.)

It is an immense joy to work together with the Blessed Virgin so that the light of God transfigure the world.

OUR ADDRESSES

FRANCE: "Enfants de Medjugorje", 15, rue Joseph le Brix, 76800 ST. ETIENNE DU ROUVRAY

BELGIUM: "Enfants de Medjugorje" chez Mr Lisin, 45 b Route d'Ellemelle, 4557 SENY - Ph. 85-51-17-94 - Cpte Nr. 634-40-100-01-93

SWITZERLAND: "Enfants de Medjugorje" chez Mr Jambers, Chemin des Harroz, 3966 RECHY - CCP: 19-52-00-1 ou Banque Cantonale du Valais Cpte Nr. 01-667-974-9 (CHALAIS)

All checks are made to "Enfants de Medjugorje".

---

[1]This address is an April fool's. Yes, but it is also a way to show that this news is entirely informal, a little newspaper on the side transmitted by a simple nun, without any pretentions to represent any official, militaray, parish or ecclesiastic solicitation whatever. It is to my family that I address myself, even if this family has increased to thousands of people... which I greet with affection!

APPENDIX IV

The Church and Medjugorje: What one should know

At present there currently is a certain blur in the spirit of the French with respect to the position of the Church regarding Medjugorje and that is easily explained. In France, more than elsewhere, the newspapers have opted for a negative prism on Medjugorje, filtering only ambiguous information and especially remaining silent about objective truths, yet circulated in other countries. What we propose doing is to present some basic points for the understanding of these facts here.

* After having adhered to the testimony of the six visionaries at the beginning of the apparitions, Monsignor Zanic (Bishop of Mostar) changed his mind and denied the authenticity of these apparitions. Put in charge of the Commission of Inquiry by Rome in as much as bishop of the place, he stated a negative judgement in 1986 to Cardinal Ratzinger. This judgement had repercussions in the newspapers and a number of Christians, even among the clergy, rested there.

* Cardinal Ratzinger rejected these negative conclusions. And an unprecedented fact in the history of the apparitions, the local bishop (Monsignor Zanic) was released of his file. This fact was hidden by the French newspapers. Rome then dissolved the commission in order to entrust the charge to a Yugoslav Episcopal Conference. The new commission was born then under the presidency of Monsignor Komarica (from Banja Luka).

* In 1985 Professor Joyeux, known worldwide, conducted scientific tests on

the visionaries in ecstasy. His documents, shown among others in a video, definitely discarded the thesis of witchcraft on the part of the visionaries or that of psychic disequilibrium.

* As it is in any other place of apparitions, neither condemned nor recognized by the church, private pilgrimages are authorized (organized by Lay people whatever the number of participants be) and official pilgrimages are not authorized (organized by bishops or priests). Of course, bishops or priests can join private pilgrimages as participants. This is a current practice.

* Yet Medjugorje, according to the number of communions distributed each day, is one of the first places of pilgrimage in the world. In 1990 more than 30,000 priests and bishops went there and many among them were encouraged by the Pope.

* On November 21, 1990, Monsignor Komarica (President of the Commission) himself came to celebrate the Mass of pilgrimage and announced that other bishops of the commission would follow. In the practice of the Church, that is equivalent to a recognition of the worship and pilgrimage. In his homily he emphasizes the good fruits of prayer and conversion in Medjugorje. "The commission recognized these fruits."

* On November 28, 1990, a text was sent to Rome. "On the basis of research conducted until now, the supernatural character of the apparitions and revelations has been established..." This text was private in a certain context, and the bishops of the commission did not design it for the public since it was not definitive. An indiscretion published it, producing great confusion. Now this formula is ambiguous. If a researcher says: "I did not establish the formula of vaccination against aids" some would say "we will never have it!", and others "it will come; patience!"

* On April 11, 1991 in Zadar the Episcopal Conference accepted Medjugorje as a place of prayer. It is not yet a final "yes" on the part of the church but it is a big "yes". In any case it is an explicit encouragement to pilgrimages and to priests to come and administer the sacraments.

* On June 17, 1991, the commission formed a "Pastoral and Liturgical Conference" whose responsibility was to help the Franciscans respect Catholic doctrine in the sanctuary. Since then this conference has not demanded any modification in the local pastoral. This is equivalent to an acquiescence of what is going on there. This conference was formed by four bishops and four theologians.

* In September 1991, at the time of the conference in Vienna, Cardinal Ratzinger declared that no definitive position had been taken by the church up to that day. "We are open. The commission continues its work. It is necessary to wait and pray."

* We can say that at present the sanctuary of Medjugorje enjoys an ecclesiastic situation analogous to that of the Rue du Bac: official recognition of the place of worship, non-recognition of the apparitions.

For Fatima or Lourdes, the waiting was also long... And in Medjugorje, the apparitions still continue! Let us pray in confidence.

(Excerpt from the Review "Les Enfants de Medjugorje, num. 11)

TABLE OF CONTENTS

Preface of Father Slavko 7
Monthly Message of the Blessed Virgin of March 25, 1992 9

I. Beginning of April: War breaks out in Bosnia-Herzegovina 11
That evening 11
News of April 7 17
To stay or to leave News of April 8 17
News of April 9 19
Six bombs and three children 20
Inspection in Citluk 21
News of April 10 22
Private fax to Florence 24
Hello, Ephraim? 24
News of April 11 25
Private fax to Vincent 26
Medjugorje-Rome by way of Paris 27

II. Mid-April, 1992: A Holy Week unlike the others 29
News of April 12 29
A Jewish mother 30
News of April 13 32
Private fax to Jean-Marc 32

Vicka and fear 33
News of April 14 33
Private fax to Geneviève 35
Private fax to Vincent 35
Interview with Vicka 36
News of April 15 36
Truly courageous? 37
News of April 16 38
Private fax to Geneviève 39
Family letter addressed to our supporters 40
The bells of the night 41
News of April 17 42
Life after life? 43
News of April 19 45
Interview with Ivan 46
Private fax to Nathalie 48
Interview with Father Jozo 48
Walk to Ljubuski 53
Monthly message of the Blessed Virgin of April 25, 1992 54
A message obtained after a great struggle 55
News of April 27 56

III May, 1992 ...What are Europe and the United Nations doing? 59
False news 59
News of May 1 60
When St. Joseph drives a Peugeot 61
Private fax to Geneviève 63
Private fax to Gildas 63
News of May 4 64
News of May 7 65
News of May 8 66
News of May 9 67
Private fax to Gildas 68
News of May 11 68
Private fax to Cyrille 69
Interview with Marija 70
Private fax to Geneviève 73
News of May 15 73
They do not have any more wine 74
News of May 19 76

The Serbian Army... the slave ship 78
The children will overcome hatred 79
Monthly message of the Blessed Virgin of May 25, 1992 81
News of May 28 81
The incense of the enemy 83

IV. June, 1992: Testimony of love from poor and little 87
News of June 1 87
Private fax to Milona 89
Some toothpaste? 89
News of June 7 90
Vukovar 1992 91
Private fax to Pascal 91
News of June 12 92
Private fax to Florence 93
News of June 15 94
One must take the rough with the smooth 95
News of Jun 19 96
But Jesus said to them: "Give them yourselves to eat" 97
Private fax to Vincent 98
News of June 23 99
Monthly message of the Blessed Virgin of June 25, 1992 100
News of June 28 101
Father Jozo meets John Paul II 102

V. July 1992: Hope against all hope 105
The candles of death 105
News of July 3 106
News of July 15 107
News of July 22 108
Monthly message of the Blessed Virgin of July 25, 1992 109
News of July 29 110

VI. August 1992: Shout out from the rooftops what takes place in secret 113
News of August 5, 1992 113
The Gospa in the corridors of French Television Channel 3 115
News of August 12 117
News of August 19 118
Monthly message of the Blessed Virgin of August 25, 1992 119

News of August 26 119

VII. September 1992: Father, forgive them... for they do not know what they do 121
News of September 2 121
A way to make peace 122
News of September 9 123
News of September 16 124
Satan was crying 126
News of September 23 127
Monthly message of the Blessed Virgin of September 25, 1992 128
News of September 30 129

VIII. October/November 1992: with Mary... from darkness to light 131
The wooden cookstove 131
News of October 15 133
Monthly message of the Blessed Virgin of October 25, 1992 134
The anti-bomb cloud 134
It is so easy at times 137
News of November 1 138
The best way to stop wars? 139
News of November 15 141
Monthly message of the Blessed Virgin of November 25, 1992 142

IX.Winter-Spring, 1992-'93 143
Persevere 143
News from Medjugorje, December 1, 1992. 143
News from Medjugorje, December 15, 1992. 144
Monthly message, December 25, 1992. 146
News from Medjugorje, January 1, 1993. 146
Revelation to Jelena, January 2, 1993. 148
News from Medjugorje, January 15, 1993. 148
Monthly message, January 25, 1993. 150
News from Medjugorje, February 17, 1993. 150
Monthly message, February 25, 1993. 151
News from Medjugorje, March 1, 1993. 151
News from Medjugorje, March 15, 1993. 153
I was four years old and I saw her. 154
Monthly message, March 25, 1993. 157
News from Medjugorje, April 1, 1993. 157

News from Medjugorje, April 15, 1993. 158
Monthly message, April 25, 1993. 159
News from Medjugorje, May 1, 1993. 160

Author's Note 163

In Conclusion 165

APPENDIX I 169
APPENDIX II 173
APPENDIX III 175
APPENDIX IV 179